MW01028289

CHANGING DIRECTION

Ten Choices That Impact Your Dreams

BY MARY MILLER

With Dustin S. Klein

SMART BUSINESS® BOOKS
An Imprint of Smart Business® Network Inc.

Changing Direction
COPYRIGHT © 2016 Mary Miller

Published by:
Smart Business Network
835 Sharon Drive, Suite 200
Westlake, OH 44145

Printed in the United States of America
Cover design: Eric R. Galinger, Galinger Graphics
Interior design: April Grasso

ISBN: 978-0-9911081-0-7
Library of Congress Control Number: 2016936268

To all the dreamers looking for a way to become the person they are meant to be today and tomorrow.

For those who have stopped dreaming, this is a place to re-engage with your dreams and excitement for the future.

CONTENTS

PROLOGUE
Changing Direction: 10 Choices
That Impact Your Dreams

"Begin with the end in mind."
—Stephen Covey

Who loves to clean toilets and mop floors? Probably not too many people, but at its most basic level, that is the service that JANCOA, the company I own with my husband Tony, provides.

In life, there is much more to a job than the actual task you do. There is much more to a livelihood and career than the job description presented to you on the first day of work. The reality is much deeper: We all want what we do to be meaningful—both for others and ourselves. Without meaning, you are lost, lacking focus, purpose, and direction. Once you have lost your way, your life can feel out of control. You feel lost, desperate. It does not have to be this way. You can change direction.

Changing direction is the story of my life. It is the story of my great transformation and learning the importance of embracing change in order to become a new me. I discovered there are 10 choices anyone can make to become a new, more energized person. My life is now dedicated to inspiring others who want to take control of their lives, embrace change, and set out on a path that leads somewhere amazing, special, and meaningful.

This is what I love to do—help people like you realize what they already know but are afraid to do anything about. More often than not, our instincts are correct. If you're unhappy, you probably know why. What you need are tools you can use to change direction, take control, and undergo your own great transformation.

This book invites you to look at my personal life journey and that of our company to see this in action. My hope is that you will see yourself in my story and learn to change direction in your own life. My journey started when I took charge of my life. Then, a few years later, Tony and I were able to change the direction of our business. Because of these changes, my life mission is drastically different and JANCOA is much more than the janitorial services firm it used to be. Today, I help others, and Tony and I together create value for our employees and clients. We create purpose and provide direction. For us, cleaning is the platform we use to instill meaning and help change lives. That's not how the company started out, but this book is not really about JANCOA or Mary Miller, it is about changing direction. It is a guide that lays out the 10 important choices you can take to change your life based on lessons I've learned from my own journey.

As you read this book, you'll discover how JANCOA helped change my life direction. Being a part of this company allowed me to undergo a significant transformation. I was able to leave behind a victim mentality that plagued the younger me—a then 30-year-old single mother of three. I met my life partner, and together we changed the way his family company did business and impacted others' lives. We embraced change and took authority over our own destiny. Then, I began to pay it forward by showing others how they could do the same. This was no easy journey, but it was worth every ache and pain suffered along the way.

Part of this great transformation came through a gradual self-realization that I didn't have all the answers. My journey led me to become a lifelong learner. This changed the way I thought, acted, and felt about myself. Part of my personal transformation came through my relationship with Tony, but the common thread is JANCOA, which has served as the platform to implement change and as a way to take lessons learned and help others achieve the same results. Without JANCOA, none of this would have been possible.

Because of this, JANCOA became something bigger for many more people than just myself. It became an organization where change and life betterment are today part of the fabric of our being. Change is ingrained in our corporate culture, and we have transformed ourselves into an employer-of-choice in our region and a national model for others to imitate. More importantly, it allowed me to branch out and help people outside of the company learn how to do what we have done. I became a public speaker and coach, presenting lessons on ways to change direction in one's life—and telling my story and JANCOA's story as proof that dreams really can come true.

Everyone has the power to change direction in his or her own world and business. You have the same ability I have to make a difference—even if you have not yet realized it.

So where does this story begin? Well, neither my awakening nor our awakening at JANCOA came in one swift eureka moment. It happened gradually, over time, as we began to recognize what changing direction meant. For JANCOA, it came when we realized we wanted to be more than a service provider and do more than simply clean customers' buildings. For me, it crystallized when I recognized that being a victim was no longer acceptable.

To succeed you must start with the end in mind. With a clear destination, you can begin this amazing journey. Along the way, you will learn to act upon the 10 critical choices necessary to achieve a new you:

- Embrace change.
- Establish dreams.
- Balance expectations and reality.

- Eliminate obstacles.
- Create meaningful dialogue and relationships.
- Think positive.
- Don't underestimate the power of desire and faith.
- Capture opportunities.
- Be ethical in everything you do.
- Take care of yourself.

That's it. When you decide to make these 10 choices you will be taking the first steps toward achieving a new you. While this may sound easy, changing direction will not happen overnight. It is a journey. There will be twists and turns, ups and downs. Throughout this book you will learn about these 10 choices and how to approach them. To demonstrate that anything is possible, I'll also pull back the curtain on my life and share insights—lessons learned, mistakes made, inspiration found. Hopefully, it will provide perspective on the journey and help you sort out the challenges you may face along the way.

During our transformation, Tony and I had numerous conversations about what we wanted. We knew that we wanted to be significant and to make a difference. We knew we wanted to provide more for our employees than just a paycheck. Through trial-and-error we stumbled toward a solution.

As a result, the JANCOA of today is much different than the JANCOA of a decade ago. Our team members do not approach the work we do with a clock-in, clock-out mentality. Everyone knows cleaning buildings is our duty—it is the job our clients pay us to do. Beyond that, JANCOA has become a springboard for something much greater than Tony and I ever imagined.

Before I explain how we underwent our transformation—and how you can get started and apply the lessons we learned—it's important to consider what it is you truly want and the path on which you want to set your life. In life, each day is part of an adventure. At the end of the day, you have the opportunity to be full of gratitude and reflection, and learn how to be the best version of yourself. Faith or intention alone does not get you what you want. Each and every one of us has to take the initiative in our lives to get what we want, and not wait for anyone else to do it for us. That is what makes us stronger and more grateful. It allows us to achieve things that are important.

When people ask me what JANCOA stands for, I explain that we are an industry transformer. We are innovators and a source of inspiration for our people. Our company has become a place of encouragement where employees can tap into resources to improve themselves in every aspect of their lives.

Of course, we also want to be the provider-of-choice for large facilities in Greater Cincinnati requiring janitorial services and an employer-of-choice for people seeking employment. We are, after all, a for-profit business.

For our clients, that means we strive to exceed expectations by practicing what we preach—going beyond simply doing a good job. We say what we mean and mean what we say. We stand behind those words.

For our employees, that means providing resources. We have developed a series of programs and initiatives that differentiate us from other companies. Foremost among these is our groundbreaking Dream Manager program, which has received national notoriety over the years, including Matthew Kelly's New York Times best-selling book, *The Dream Manager*, as well as training programs and keynotes—including a TED talk—that have derived from it.

In his book, Kelly portrays JANCOA as a fictional company (Admiral Janitorial Services) helping employees achieve their dreams and thereby serving as an example for other companies to achieve success. In real life, our Dream Manager program is designed to help employees reach life goals, such as purchasing a home, learning to speak English, becoming a better parent, improving finances, or other personal aspirations that have been as different as the people who work for us. Learning how to speak English has actually been a very popular dream people have wanted to realize—that's because a whopping 57 percent of our team members are Hispanic.

We have employees that represent more than 20 different countries. Together, these groups make up 70 percent of our team, and every one of them came to America with the dream of achieving a better quality of life for their families.

Yet in spite of our successes it has not been a straight-line journey to get here. I have made many mistakes and had several setbacks along the way. I promise not to sugar coat my story in the pages ahead. I am a completely different person than I used to be. I don't say this to toot my own horn, but to demonstrate that if I can do it, you can too. These are hard lessons learned, such as understanding how to focus on making positive change in the areas that I could impact. This required learning how to let go of the guilt and stress that I cannot own and realizing that all of the people in my life—my grandparents, parents, previous bosses, school teachers—did the best job they could do for me.

If you want to change direction, you have to do the same thing. You can't blame anyone else for your past mistakes. For me, this meant marrying the wrong person, not getting a college degree, and leaving my children at home while I worked to make ends meet. Like me, you are responsible for your life. You can write a new script and follow it.

Several years ago, during a five-day retreat I attended, my "aha" moment was when I realized that my current situation was due to the way I perceived my experience from the past. I thought of my children and how my choices during their childhood may have created problems in their current lives. I called them that morning and told them, "I'm sorry for anything in your life I did that caused you pain, suffering, anxiety, or that hurt you in any way."

My son said to me, "Mom, you never did anything but love me and want the best for me."

Today, I have a beautiful and meaningful relationship with my children because we can talk openly about our feelings, goals, the pressures we feel, and how we can help each other. We raise each other up. This is what I hope my experiences can help you learn.

Some days, I still can't believe this is what my life has become. In the late 1990s, a friend invited me to a YWCA Career Women of Achievement luncheon where her company sponsored a table. I had no idea what to expect. Up until that point in my life, I had focused on raising my children and struggling to make ends meet. As I sat in that room—with 500 women (and a couple men)—I listened to the astounding success stories being told. It was truly moving. I remember wondering: How incredible would it be to achieve that type of recognition and have that type of strength to overcome obstacles?

I became a voracious reader and read any business book I could get my hands on that might bring fresh ideas to our company—books about managing people, finances, sales, marketing, inspirational leaders, and faith. Knowledge can become addictive. Today, my e-reader has more books on it than I could possibly digest in my downtime. This is a good thing. The more you read, the more you can walk in others' footsteps and learn from their experiences.

My ultimate hope is that this book feeds your mind with the same type of knowledge I sought, but is instilled with enough positivity so that you feel equipped with the resources necessary to change direction and embrace every significant moment in your life. Experiences are really nothing more than life's little building blocks. Ultimately, you are the architects for your own futures. It requires some planning and effort. Starting is simple. You just have to take the first step toward changing direction of your life. That journey can start right now when you decide to turn the page.

CHAPTER 1
Embrace Change

"To help create positive change in others,
you must first find the catalyst for positive change in yourself."
—Mary Miller

Tony once told a friend: "If you want to watch the sun rise, you won't see it if you face west." I overheard him share this bit of wisdom many years ago with someone looking for a bit of inspiration. I have since taken that sage piece of wisdom and expanded it, using it in many of my coaching and/or speaking events, by sharing that it doesn't take a lot more money, education, or planning to get what you want. All you have to do is simply look in a different direction to get the result you are looking for in life.

Tony's quick thinking and seemingly simple statement was offering much more than a nugget of advice. It became a moment of clarity for me. I think of that statement frequently and the difference it made to me. When we look back on our past experiences and realize each one is a step in the journey to changing direction it's clear that we must embrace change.

If you want anything relevant from life—whether it's as basic as seeing the sun rise or as complex as closing a multimillion-dollar deal—you need to view change as a good thing rather than something to avoid. Knowing which direction to face must be a conscious and deliberate decision, and one you're committed to following through.

Before JANCOA, I never thought of myself as an entrepreneur or a leader, and certainly not someone who could inspire others. I was just trying to figure out who I was and putting out the fires that broke out each day of my life. Raising three children and working full time left no time for "exploring self." Developing a career was the last thing on my mind. Earning enough to meet our household needs was my main focus, and I did that well. Situations change, and you either change with them or get left behind. Embracing change requires you to commit fully to whatever it is you want, and then work tirelessly to make it happen. You are the only one who can change direction. No one will do it for you. If you keep your eyes and ears open, your experiences will provide the answers and knowledge you need to build that better future. For a long time, I thought everyone else had the answers and that success came from pleasing other people. Boy, was I wrong.

> Knowing which direction to face must be a conscious and deliberate decision that you're willing to follow through on to the end.

Despite that, I had a lot of good things going for me that I hadn't yet recognized: I'm an extrovert, as well as a natural salesperson who easily warms up to others because I truly enjoy people. These traits proved critical to my personal change story. However, I ignored those skills, and instead tried to succeed by making others happy. This tactic only produced short-term results and did little to build a strong foundation for my family's future. Like others who find themselves in a tough place in life, I needed something, a spark to serve as the catalyst for my transformation. That came when I attended a life-changing seminar that allowed me to press the reset button on my life. This wouldn't have happened if I hadn't embraced change. I also met Tony through this seminar program, and I believe I saw the possibilities of a great relationship with someone else who was embracing change and focusing on achieving a bigger future.

Today, my life is filled with happiness and joy, as well as confidence to overcome the obstacles that try to steal that joy. I don't strive for perfection, but feel 80 percent is a great goal (giving myself mercy and grace). I eat well—as healthy as possible; sleep well—seven to eight hours each night; exercise—my best days start with walking my dog and feeding my mind—taking in information, reading and listening to books, broadcasts, and music. Back in 1987 (which happened to be the year I turned 30!), and many of the years before, my life was far from positive, and my laugh was far from genuine.

Ask yourself:

- Are you facing opportunity and promise?
- Is this something you care enough about to both see the opportunity and seize it?
- Or, are you focused on—and reacting to—past disappointments and willing to just get by?
- Do you embrace change or run from it?

My chance encounter with Tony was really just the beginning. The seminar where I met him opened my eyes to what I was doing wrong in life and how I was looking at life in general. I stopped focusing on being a people pleaser. I learned how to speak up and take a stand for what I believed in. I recognized how to own my responsibilities without assuming responsibility for every person and every problem. This was an awakening, but one that shouldn't have come as a surprise considering the road that led me here.

Years earlier, when I was 17, I got pregnant and had to finish high school the summer after my junior year. Two years later, I was a divorcee and single parent—not exactly the start to life anyone imagines they'll have.

Life throws a lot at you. You can buckle under the pressure or take what comes your way and do the most with it. I chose the latter and found a way to provide for my family.

My so-called business career started rather unimpressively with an entry-level clerical job at a major footwear corporation. For the next 10 years I worked hard, rising through the ranks to become the manager of sales operations with a team of six people to manage all functions for the division—from processing orders to customer service. It was a good job with a lot of responsibility, and I was happy. Along the way, I married—and divorced—again. That didn't matter as much. My world had become much more stable, and my life settled into what most would call a normal routine.

They say that all good things must come to an end. My world came crashing down in 1987 when my division closed. There wasn't much to be positive about back then. With no college degree to fall back on, my options were limited. Failure wasn't an option. Instead, I focused on doing whatever it took to survive. In life, you need to discover what you're exceptional at and match it with what makes you happy. There is a magical balance between the two, and when you find it, your life will be filled with meaning. That's what happened when I recognized my talent for sales. It turned out that I had an innate ability to listen, connect with people, and speak honestly. Those are important traits that provide a solid foundation in sales. Just as important, I liked sales. So with the right formula for success in place I took a big risk and accepted a 100 percent commission-based job. There weren't many opportunities available for me, but I believed in myself and my ability to persevere.

Within a few months, my faith and hard work paid off and I was promoted to business manager. My boss, who saw a lot of potential in me, became my unofficial mentor and started guiding me toward becoming a more professional businessperson. This was my first real attempt to embrace change with open arms.

Around that time I read Dr. Norman Vincent Peale's *The Power of*

Positive Thinking and began to think seriously about my future.

Roadblocks come in many disguises. The key is recognizing what they are and identifying ways to overcome them. You can go around them, over them, under them, and even right through them—it all depends on your approach, and it is all part of the adventure.

Faith has been an important part of my life. It helped me through my darkest days, and there were lots of those. Once my new mentor demonstrated his confidence in my abilities—and me—it gave me renewed strength. It's truly astonishing what can happen when you encourage others. One way he did this was investing in training. He sent me to continuing education programs that allowed me to hone

> Spark passion by asking questions that reveal a vision of the future you want.

my skills. Then he sent me to a series of life and business training seminars. It was at one of these seminars where I first met Tony Miller.

Tony was a 39-year-old entrepreneur who was running his business, JANCOA. It was a small cleaning company that employed two full-time people who worked in the office, and some part-time staff who handled the janitorial duties. Tony was attending the seminar in hopes of getting a boost for both his life and business. The two of us immediately hit it off.

Tony's story was drastically different than my own. As a 19-year-old student at the University of Cincinnati, he noticed how dirty the floors were at the bars he frequented. Tony thought to himself, "I can clean these floors to pay my tab." So, he founded JANCOA.

The fledgling enterprise grew steadily and helped him pay the bills. Then, his father went into the hospital for open-heart surgery and passed away during recovery. As a result, Tony left school to support his mother and three siblings. JANCOA became their salvation.

Fast-forward 20 years: The two of us met at this seminar and Tony promised to take me to lunch, but life seemingly gets in the way of such things. We both got busy and lunch never happened. One year later, however, serendipity changed the course of things once more. I ran into Tony again—this time at a mutual friend's wedding. He had a date, but that didn't stop me from approaching him. There had been a spark when we met at the seminar, and I knew it. So I interrupted Tony's date and playfully reminded him that he still owed me lunch. I didn't know if he would remember, or even still want to go out, but I wasn't letting this opportunity pass me by without giving it a try.

As it turns out, Tony had been thinking about me, too, and we ended up going out on that lunch date.

Fate's a funny thing. Tony jokes to this day that he knew I was trouble from the beginning. Of course, I had heard the same stories about him. So I guess we were meant for each other. We both had challenging pasts. We both endured failed relationships. We had children. Yet, we are both hard-working individuals who never settle. Most importantly, we both were willing to embrace change. That was the common thread—we were owning our lives and changing direction.

I still remember the day when I fell in love with Tony. He invited my children and me to visit his lake house for the weekend. He was there with his best friend—who to this day still works with us at JANCOA— and eight children from their church who had never been out on a lake, or even to the country.

These children were staying with Tony for the weekend. He was taking them out on his boat, teaching them to fish, making s'mores, and generally giving them a great weekend. Watching this, I saw Tony in a completely different light. Here was someone busy with a growing business and other initiatives, yet he was taking time to help improve the lives of children who weren't even his. It was then that I recognized Tony for who he really is: a man with a heart bigger than the world. I was blown away, and it was then that I knew I wanted to be part of his life and for him to be part of mine. He would be my future husband. We married two years after that first lunch date.

If you want to improve your life, learn to take charge of your choices. If you're not happy, ask questions that reveal a vision of the future you want, one that helps capture your passion. Stop blaming others for the situation you're in. Then, run as fast as you can toward the change you want to create and leave your old self's thought process behind.

During the late spring of 1993, I was still working at my sales job. Neither Tony nor I had yet considered that I would come to work at JANCOA. Then, my boss decided that I would start working on Sundays. My job supplied a nice income for our family—money we needed—and I was very good at it. Plus, I liked what I was doing. Sundays? No way! That simply wasn't going to work for our family. Tony and I decided it was time for another change: I would leave the sales job and start working in the family business. This was a big, scary decision. I made more money than JANCOA brought in for our household, so this was a huge leap of faith. Our relationship and family's quality of life was far more important than the guarantee of a certain income level. So, in May 1993, I joined JANCOA.

At the time, the company was doing about $2 million a year. We had 65 part-time employees and an employee turnover rate of nearly 380 percent—a number that surprisingly isn't unusual for the janitorial industry. My initial responsibilities involved running operations, addressing our personnel problems, and meeting regularly with clients to make sure they were happy. While we were hovering at the industry average for turnover, Tony and I never aspire to be average. On any given night we were short about 35 employees. Our team members— at least the ones who showed up—were being overworked to pick up the slack. We didn't realize how much a strain it was, so we figured we'd just keep grinding away—sometimes as much as 80 hours a week—in order to get by. We would resolve our people issue by hiring more people. People, however, are the engine that keeps any business running smoothly. Keeping people was JANCOA's biggest problem. Fixing that problem became my mission, but being new to this world, I really didn't know where to start.

Part of embracing change is recognizing how to ask the right questions to ease your concerns and provide guidance on the next steps you need to take. I figured the answers lay with the people we served—our customers—so I started visiting them and asking whether they were getting top-line service from our team members. Stretched or not, we couldn't let the company lose sight of its clients' needs. As this happened, I quickly realized JANCOA had the potential to be so much more than it was.

Two months later, on July 7, 1993, I worked my first 26-hour day. When I arrived home, Tony was waiting up for me…and smiling. He was so happy that somebody else was willing to work as hard as he was in the business. It's because of this common commitment that we were able

> **Do you embrace change or run from it?**

to buckle down and fix JANCOA's problems. We hired a consultant to help us become a better company. Our thinking was that if we could simply turn off the faucet and hire more people, we would overcome the personnel shortages we faced. If we focused on that, the consultant could provide us with a game plan to grow the company.

He came to Cincinnati to do a deep dive into our company. We thought he would analyze our processes, systems, and other methods we used to run the company and offer recommendations on how to improve. We envisioned his guidance to build a plan for growth. Instead, on the second day after arriving in Cincinnati, the consultant fired us.

"I can't help you," he said. "You have a people problem. Until you address that, you'll never be able to grow this business."

At first, we were devastated. Then we realized he was right. It was a real eye opener and set us on the right path: Our solution wasn't strength in numbers and attracting more people to the company. Rather, it was attracting and retaining the right people by changing our company's culture and focusing on our people. Our soul searching began. If we wanted the best people to work for JANCOA, what did that look like? If we wanted our employees to be successful, how would we train them? If we wanted to retain engaged team members, what would it take?

Tony and I agreed we wanted people to work at JANCOA for three to five years, and then leave to pursue their dreams. Research showed that most people who work for cleaning companies view their jobs as a transition; the type you take while you're looking for something else that provides better upward mobility. We concluded that if we developed programs that took care of our people better we could improve employee satisfaction and, as a result, longevity.

There comes a moment in everyone's life where they face a crossroads that has the potential to dramatically alter the course of their future. This was JANCOA's: Could we effectively recognize where we were and clearly identify where we wanted to go, and why? What would it take to deliberately and systematically overhaul the business? Most important, were we committed to overcoming the stumbling blocks and challenges we knew stood in the way of achieving these goals? We knew we had to be all-in on this journey or it would fail.

First, we had to change the perspective of how we saw the company. We had to view JANCOA as more than simply a cleaning service. It's amazing. When you focus beyond yourself or your industry—or in our case beyond simply mopping floors and cleaning toilets—you start to recognize that you can offer others so much more. We had been wearing blinders for years. Our ultimate business purpose became taking care of people: our people, their families, and our clients' people. Tony and

I recognized that if we opened the lines of communication with our team and showed them how cleaning toilets created an opportunity for them to make impactful changes in their lives, it would fundamentally change our company—and their lives—for the better.

By investing in people, they would want to work harder for our customers and look for ways to create more value in the work they did each day. Our team members would feel better about themselves as they grew their careers, building a common groundswell of ownership and pride across the company. Our employees were members of our family. By treating them like family members, we hit upon a creative solution that would fundamentally transform JANCOA and our employees' lives.

As a young adult, I had no idea the sun was rising behind me. Now, with Tony by my side, its glow was beginning to materialize. Business guru and author Peter Drucker said, "Too often, businesses put people on the liability side as a cost on their spreadsheet or their statement versus on the asset side." He was right. When you are in the service industry, your product is your people. For Tony and me, embracing change meant offering the same road map we were developing for our lives to our people so they could also realize the promise of tomorrow we were working toward. This was a significant shift in the way we looked at our employees. Today, our employees see how they can reach their goals and change the lives of others. They want to be a part of our culture and enjoy the opportunities JANCOA provides. Together, we learned how to shift our perspectives so we could see and embrace life's possibilities.

The results have been nothing less than amazing. Today, JANCOA's annual sales exceed $15 million. We employ more than 500 full-time people. Our turnover rate is 300 percent better than the national average. Part of this transformation can be attributed to our mindset change. Much of it is due to new programs we designed to make JANCOA an employer-of-choice, chief among them our Dream Manager program, which has given employees the tools to do better for themselves in life and, along the way, inspired a national best-selling book.

By embracing change I also came to view my role through a different lens: The most important job of any CEO is to ensure your team understands your company vision and to provide future opportunities for each and every one of them. When employees believe success can happen for them professionally and personally, they begin to dream about the future.

That idea of achieving what's seemingly out of reach is something anyone can integrate into their life—no matter their circumstances. Think about it: How often do you face west all day, every day? How many people just plug away at work and go through the motions at home? Why do people wait for something big to happen instead of going out and doing it? Why do we let fate rest in someone else's hands rather than our own?

The answer is simple: People do not commit themselves fully to what it is they want. Often, fear prevents people from moving forward. When

Help people realize the promise of tomorrow by offering employees the same road map you develop for your life.

you succumb to fear, even though you have everything you need to succeed at your disposal, you might still miss out on extraordinary opportunities because you continue to do the same old thing. It's like Yoda said in "The Empire Strikes Back," "Do or do not; there is no try." There is definitely an intentionality at work when you decide to do one thing different today from how you did it yesterday. Something magical happens.

There is something magnetic about an inspired, excited individual: Their eyes dance and they're full of hope. When they see numerous possibilities in life suddenly open up before them, their whole body changes. They sit up straighter, they stand a little taller—they're practically floating. Their face glows as their heart beats faster and they realize that there is more to life than a daily grind.

It's funny to think about my personal experience with this. Both Tony and I grew up in the school of hard knocks and experienced a series of life-changing events that shifted our perspective and turned us toward the east. We had no idea that our transformation would lead us toward helping the very people who worked with us so they could begin their own transformations. We changed the way we treated each day. We altered the way we ran our business. We shifted the way we looked at our people. It turned out that we had the resources we needed all along. Together we learned, gradually, how to face the sunrise. We appreciated its beauty, drew energy, and saw opportunity in each day's new beginning. It was possible because together we embraced change in all aspects of our life.

CHAPTER 2
Establish Dreams

"A dream doesn't become reality through magic;
it takes sweat, determination and hard work."
—Gen. Colin Powell

Something extraordinary happens when you allow yourself to dream. It opens the door to endless possibilities about what the future can be. Do you remember how exciting and wonderful it was when you were a child and dreamt about your future self? Did you dream about becoming a dancer, inventor, scientist, or professional athlete? Did you dream about getting your driver's license and cruising along behind the wheel of a shiny sports car? We all have dreams. Everyone has something he or she wants to pursue. Each one of us is born with dreams along with the talents and abilities to achieve those dreams.

Dreaming has a ripple effect: It starts with a single person with an idea about what the future could be. Then, by working to make that idea reality, the dream begins to take on a life of its own. It's a magical thing. Unfortunately, something happens as we grow up—many of us no longer take the time to dream.

There are several reasons for this: Sometimes, it's because we are surrounded by too many depressing things in the world—poverty, hunger, war, terrorism—and there simply isn't enough positive energy to fuel the possibility of achieving dreams as there should be. Other times, one person stymies another. Consider the parent who says, "My daughter has this crazy dream!" and is so fearful that their child will get hurt, that rather than encouraging her dreams, squashes them. Too often, people find themselves lacking the courage or positive encouragement to dream. They become too timid to change their life direction and too weak to do what it takes to make their dreams reality.

What if more people established and pursued dreams? What if there was more positive encouragement across all levels that spurred more people to dream? Think about how wonderful the world would be. Think about the many opportunities present when people support each other's dreams and encourage more dreaming. Great things happen when you are empowered to take charge of your life, change direction, and start dreaming. Some of us just need permission or that extra push to get started.

Beyond lacking encouragement, another obstacle sometimes blocks our ability to dream—being programmed to approach dreams based on our own life experiences. People are reluctant to stretch themselves to think outside their comfort zone. When I was a single mom and at the lowest point in life, all I wanted was to get a job so I could pay the rent and support my children. Everything around me was falling apart, so my dreams were modest and practical. I had a clear vision about what I wanted, but I still had pictures on my refrigerator of my dream car—a convertible—and my dream home. I had those big, far away dreams of how I wanted my life to be, and that got me through the tough times. Too many people stop dreaming about what life could be and just focus on survival. It doesn't have to be that way. The size of your bank account or level of education doesn't matter when it comes to dreaming. Everyone has disappointment; everyone faces struggles; but this is no reason to stop dreaming. When you stop dreaming, you stop being engaged in your life and start going through the motions. That's no way to live.

It's very important to have something big to work toward. Without dreams, you live with mediocrity and settle for what you have—with regret. Worse, with no dreams, you have no direction in life. What could be sadder than that? So how can you be happier and learn how to start dreaming again? How can you reinvigorate your life by relearning how to establish those dreams you had from your youth?

Start with this simple exercise: Look at your life today and think about the future, five or 10 years from now. What do you want your life to look like? How do you want to be happy? Changing direction means recognizing that what you're doing now isn't what you intend to do in the future. You can't base your dreams on where you are today in life. If you do, you will only continue the cycle you're in, and for too many people, that's survival mode. Think beyond the walls that contain you and start dreaming about what's possible.

> Build a list of things you're excited about and each day review whether you took one step toward making any of them reality.

My breakthrough came while I was in a workshop and the facilitator asked, "If you were dead, how do you want people to remember you? What do you want people to be saying about you?" That was truly beginning with the end in mind, and for me it was an eye-opening experience. I had never thought about a legacy before this. I had been so absorbed in dealing with the here and now for so many years that it never occurred to me to think about what I could do with my life in order to leave something meaningful behind. I had never taken time to ask myself: How do I want my children, friends, and family to talk about me when I'm gone?

Mother Teresa did so many astounding things in her life that people will always remember her legacy, but you don't have to be Mother Teresa in order to dream about your legacy. I serve on numerous nonprofit boards and want to make an impact for those organizations that goes beyond me. Nobody may remember my name years from now, but I know that I'm doing things today that make a difference in people's lives. For me, that's one of my dreams come true.

Next, build a list of things you're really excited about, that you dream could happen to you. Each day, stop and think about what you're doing to move yourself in the right direction toward achieving those dreams. What are three things you can do this week to move forward? Make a plan and hold yourself accountable to follow through. Recruit a friend that you trust that would also be excited to pursue their dreams. Work together and encourage each other. Benjamin Franklin wrote, "By failing to prepare, you are preparing to fail." Without some sort of plan to move forward, without vision and a will to act, your dreams will remain just that—dreams.

A mentor, whom I met while working as a salesperson for a mobile home company, believed that you could create more than just jobs for the people who work for you. He sponsored employees to attend life-changing programs for those who wanted to improve the way they thought, felt, and acted. He encouraged people to learn how to develop better relationships, build higher confidence, and lead happier, more successful lives. He had nothing to lose and everything to gain by helping his employees improve. As a result, he watched employees create a better quality of life. He had the foresight to see that by helping people improve their lives they would be more productive in helping him achieve his business goals. It all works together. Little did I realize at the time that his encouragement to help me think differently would lead to me paying it forward with the work I do personally, as well as professionally through JANCOA.

JANCOA's Dream Manager program is a vehicle that gives people the tools and encouragement to achieve their dreams, and when good things happen to people, they want to share it. This concept is contagious. We all want to feel better about our lives, to do meaningful work—to be excited about the future and all the possibilities. The program is a philosophy along with the framework to empower people to dream and reach their goals.

We envisioned how JANCOA could open the doors of opportunity for our people and knew we'd be a better company for it. Our people would work toward life goals and fulfill their dreams, and we would help them along the way. They'd grow loyalty and we'd reduce turnover—something that had plagued the company for years. Through the Dream Manager program we would work together, on the same path forward, and this would create a more cohesive, inspired team. Working for us would benefit them beyond their paychecks.

It sounds too good to be true—of course, that's what most people think when they learn that we want to help people move on, potentially to new careers or to even start their own business. It sounds crazy to create a program that helps good people find a way out of your business. In essence, that is what JANCOA does. The Dream Manager program involves a complete life-career goal-setting exercise. We don't just encourage our employees to dream big—including dreaming beyond a job at JANCOA—we hired a specialist, a Dream Manager, to facilitate groups and meet one-on-one with team members interested in accomplishing a specific dream. He helps them walk through the wall of fear and gives guidance to paths to achieve what they want. It is important that the dreamer does the work to achieve the results they want on their own as this is what fuels the confidence to dream bigger.

So, what exactly is the Dream Manager program? Well, think about what you want in life—what do you hope to achieve? Would you go back to school? Build a new house? Pay for a child's college education? We all have dreams about how we would make our lives happier. The more mentors and friends we have cheering us on and backing us with encouragement and resources, the more likely we are to reach these goals. During the process, we enrich our lives with the experience of working together to make big changes.

We all have different goals and aspirations in life. We asked ourselves, "What are the dreams of our people? How could we help?" Originally, we thought we knew what they wanted and proceeded with our own preconceived notions. It turned out that not everyone wants to own a home or to drive. So we learned a big lesson early in the process: Ask them what they want! We asked them: "What are your dreams?" We tried creating a survey but also discovered that we weren't getting a strong response. The answers we received were very topical, and relied strongly on outside forces. One example was, "I want to win the lottery."

Some employees answered they wanted to learn to speak English (70 percent of our employees are immigrants and refugees that came to the U.S. to improve the quality of life for them and their families). Others wanted to rise in the ranks of JANCOA. Some wanted to provide for their family and afford an education to help them achieve a higher income. Buying houses, making ends meet, helping children look forward to a bigger future— these are dreams we all have. The Dream Manager program

Do you have a detailed action plan that lays out a path toward achieving your dreams? Do you have the top three dreams you want to achieve in the next 12 months?

acknowledges these goals. We realized that if JANCOA could help our people live richer lives, they would give back to our organization in the most important ways: showing up on schedule and on time, providing quality service, paying attention to detail, and caring about their work. Really, we asked very little in return for the life-changing vehicle we offered to each and every employee at every level in our organization. What we found is that the more we helped them, the more they helped us. We all felt happier, more fulfilled—and we became more successful together.

When we started asking our employees what their hopes were for the future, we received some surprising answers. We take for granted the things that make everyday life run seamlessly. Speaking English for example, or, having dependable transportation, are things many of us never think about let alone worry over. We don't think about the fact that we live in a house, but many of our employees never imagined coming up with a down payment to afford a place of their own.

As we collected the dream information, we began to see the world through the eyes of our employees. We gained a better understanding of our people problem and what was driving turnover. It wasn't that people didn't appreciate or want to work for JANCOA. Other life challenges were getting in the way of them performing their jobs. By providing more than a job—by giving our people a ticket toward reaching their goals and realizing their dreams—we could do much more than provide a job. We knew that we'd be paid back by loyalty and hard work on the part of our employees.

We took the leap and a big risk to invest (our time, treasure, and talent) in creating a program known today as the Dream Manager. First, we needed a Dream Manager—someone to meet with our employees and help them map out a plan for their dreams. We needed someone our people could trust, from field employees to upper management (the Dream Manager program was meant for all of us, including execs, and some of our customers even participated).

We developed a program that was separate from JANCOA. We felt it was important for people to trust that we want what is in their best interests. Most people struggle to accept that a company and its owners actually care about the employees. So we made the investment and hired a manager with experience in human resources, financial advising, and the personality to connect with people from all backgrounds. We found our first Dream Manager by divine intervention after talking the possibilities to death. One weekend, Tony and I decided to attend a new church. That Sunday, we ran into a friend we had not seen in years. We looked at each other and a quick look told us we were thinking the same thing: Joe would be a perfect Dream Manager. He quickly became excited about the possibility. As it turned out, we created a role that was going to fulfill a critical managerial role in JANCOA's culture and a job many of our applicants told us they saw as a dream position, a real opportunity to make a difference. I have had many people say they want to be our Dream Manager. Hearing this, we knew we were on to something. Since he was a long-time friend, we knew his character and capabilities. His community involvement and eagerness to learn and work with people sealed our belief—we knew he could apply his experience and passion in a positive way at JANCOA. He was enthusiastic and a raving fan of our fledgling program. This was incredibly important because he would ultimately be the champion and driver of the program, working at the ground level with each of our employees to help them map out the future of their dreams.

We also knew this was not going to be an easy job, and there was risk involved. What if the program didn't work?

Well, as soon as we kicked off the program, Joe scheduled workshops and quickly had one-on-one appointments about perceived obstacles to specific dreams. Employees wanted to sit down and talk about their dreams. There was a seismic shift in employee attitude. For most of them, this was the first time someone had asked them about their dreams and offered to help. Many of them had never considered mapping out a future. They lived day by day, paycheck to paycheck, making ends meet. I understand that struggle well because I lived it for the better part of my young adulthood. Unless someone takes your hand and shows you a better path, how will you know there's another road than the one you are taking? Our gut instinct to launch this program was spot on.

Of course, we didn't expect to make a life-changing impact on every person who worked at JANCOA. That's because the program demands total accountability on the part of employees. We provide the resources and support to set goals and reach them, but at the end of the day, they're in charge of making it happen for themselves. Sure, we helped many people create a plan to buy their first home—but we did not pay their down payment. We make English classes accessible to our employees and supply the teacher, but it's up to them to take advantage of the program—to do the work and learn.

What we found with the Dream Manager program is that our employees overwhelmingly want better lives for themselves and their families. Maybe JANCOA is a transition job to another career. Perhaps it is a job to get food on the table. Some saw themselves moving up our ladder. Others wanted to start their own businesses, sometimes cleaning companies. The Dream Manager program created an open forum for them

See the world through your employees' eyes and you will learn about their aspirations and dreams.

to discuss what they wanted out of life. Because of this, JANCOA opened opportunities for success and they valued JANCOA more. We became more than a cleaning company, and much more than a job or paycheck. We became the vehicle driving our people's dreams, and that has made all the difference in our retention rate. The Dream Manager program helped reach our potential as a company—to serve people.

After a few employees began sharing their success stories, word spread fast about the value of the Dream Manager program. One of the unique features of the program—despite being initiated by the leadership team—is that it's actually executed at ground level by our employees. It works because they generate interest among their peers in our organization by working hard to fulfill their dreams. This shows their teammates how JANCOA and the Dream Manager program played a part in that future-mapping process that ultimately changed their life direction.

We started to see more open dialogue among employees and managers because we had created a culture where everyone could learn from one another and benefit. There was more give-and-take, and more giving in general. We became more than a cleaning company, and most people felt better about working at JANCOA. So did I, because I knew that we were providing so much more for our employees than ever before. We were giving them a chance to improve their quality of life. This continues to be my greatest source of excitement and energy. I became more than just a CEO and it all began with encouraging people to establish dreams and putting a plan together to achieve their dreams.

One of the things I love most about the Dream Manager program is that it gives people permission to do what is necessary to get what they want in their lives. That's the part that is most powerful. We've had employees come from 53 different countries. We have helped more than 20 families buy homes. People have gained the strength and courage to open bank accounts, get their GEDs, learn English, and get their driver's license. One of our team members, a young man from Nigeria, came into the office one day and asked if the Dream Manager and I were in the office. He had just passed the test and gotten his first driver's license. His first job in the U.S. was at JANCOA, and now he could focus on his next dream of a higher paying job off of the bus line. He had more possibilities because of the driver's license that our Dream Manager program helped make a reality! That is what makes life exciting—helping others get excited about making their life better than it previously was.

What's amazing is that the program can be implemented with any group of people. In a business, the only caveat is that it requires supervisors and managers to work with their team rather than just being their boss. Once you've committed to it, start having dream conversations at lunch and rotate who leads the conversations. This can be as simple as having monthly brown bag luncheons. If you're bold enough, create a Dream Team to build out the program. If you empower them, this team can become very creative once given permission and boundaries on what they can and can't do within the program.

The most frequent question I receive is: "What do I have to do to be a Dream Manager?" The truth is we are all Dream Managers! There are people in our lives that we want to help achieve their dreams. Also, when you're working toward your own dreams, you don't know who is watching. There are times we encourage others without knowing it because actions really do speak louder than words. There are five key principles to being a great Dream Manager and having a successful program:

CARE: You can't pretend to care, people can tell if you are genuine.

ASK: Ask the people that you care about what they want. It was a big lesson for us to discover that what we thought they wanted was not the case at all.

LISTEN: Make sure your heart and ears are wide open. Do not assume you know what they are going to say.

ACKNOWLEDGE: Show you heard what people said by repeating it back to them. Not word for word, but integrated with the meaning of what you heard them say.

ENCOURAGE: Support people to accomplish what they tell you is important. This can be done by asking them how it is going or letting them know that you believe they can achieve the result they want.

If you follow these principles you will learn to see through their eyes and find out what is important to them rather than assuming you have all the answers. For example, offering great benefits, but not having your team use them does not help them or your company.

Today, I dream all the time and encourage everyone to do the same. Dreaming is powerful, and I talk about it through the coaching and speaking that I do, as well as in everyday conversations. Dreaming has become as much a part of me as breathing. It's such a powerful concept because people do not fight about their future dreams—they just think about them. People fight about the problems that plague their present and past, not about the dreams of the future. Integrating dreaming into your life makes me think about how a cable is created. It consists of many little ropes braided together. Your dreams are these braids interwoven to make the cable, and together those braided dreams create the energy needed to move forward toward the goals and tasks that aren't always fun and exciting. Dreaming big brings excitement that helps us move through the tough stuff we face in everyday life. Keeping a positive attitude helps us work through the obstacles that always happen along the way.

> Changing direction requires you to recognize that what you did today is part of your dreams for a better tomorrow.

Dreaming without understanding how to bring your dreams to reality isn't productive. It's crucial to recognize that once you've established your dreams you need to make sure you're willing to work to reach them, that you are committed to creating a workable plan, and learning to balance your expectations with reality. It all starts with establishing dreams. If you don't have one already, purchase a notebook or journal to be your Dream Book. Start by listing all the things you want to have and accomplish in your lifetime. Dream is a verb and you should always have an action plan to start moving in the direction of your dreams.

CHAPTER 3
Balance Expectations and Reality

"A smart man makes a mistake, learns from it,
and never makes that mistake again. But a wise man finds a smart man
and learns from him how to avoid the mistake altogether."
—Roy H. Williams

Everyone has the ability to dream. Sometimes people get so caught up in a dream that they don't recognize whether making that dream come true is feasible. That doesn't mean you shouldn't dream big—in fact, what you're able to accomplish is often much more than you ever thought possible. When setting expectations based on dreams it's important to remember to balance expectations with reality.

For example, we all have physical limitations. I might never be a world-class sprinter—no matter how hard I dream that it might come true. I could train hard enough to run a marathon, so a realistic dream might be to finish a marathon. Put another way, too often we look at somebody else's life—Richard Branson, Bill Gates, Michael Jordan, or Oprah Winfrey—and dream that we could live a life just like them. Never mind the fact that you do not have an entrepreneurial bent, high-tech computer programming skills, an athletic inclination, or the ability to easily connect with people. When you get caught up in dreams without balancing expectations and reality, it becomes a hard place to live in because you will feel disappointed and never achieve happiness.

Simply put, expectations are what you want to have in your life. The reality is knowing who you are and what talents and skills you possess to achieve the dreams important to you. That's a very important nuance because we tend to measure our success on our expectations without taking into consideration what we need to do to make it a reality. One dream that would be unrealistic for me would be winning "American Idol" and having that expectation would be very disappointing. The reality is I can't sing. When I call my grandchildren to wish them a happy birthday, they immediately request that I not sing.

This goes hand in hand with being able to change direction of your life. Many people lack direction—and they're so entrenched in their daily habits that they are not aware they lack direction. When you change direction, you can start dreaming much easier. It's like a gas tank—it can be empty, full, or somewhere in between. When the gas tank is empty, the car cannot move at all. I use this analogy to describe our energy. Think about when your energy tank is full, you have high expectations and dreams of something you are moving toward. You can move the needle from empty to full by dreaming. It's important to have high expectations, and when we live up to those expectations and start achieving what it is we want in our lives, it creates a whole new energy level and a fuller gas tank. That's why it is critical to start dreaming, find your new direction, set realistic expectations, and work toward making those dreams come true.

Think about how excited young people are when they're graduating from high school or college. They have a lot of energy and confidence about their future. They have dreams, direction, and know what they want in life. There is a deep-seeded expectation that life is going to be better than what it was when they started their education. This is a very powerful and motivational feeling.

Too often, however, events happen in people's lives that cause them to lower their expectations—even if those expectations are achievable—and then abandon their dreams. It could be some type of disappointment, hardship, or setback—the death of a relationship, financial setback, or a dream. It might be as simple as a failure to balance expectations with reality and then suddenly facing a brick wall that seems impenetrable. Because your reality is out of whack, instead of working through the obstacle, that very issue that caused it will make you stop dead in your tracks. Then, it all begins to fall apart. You stop dreaming. Your expectations change. Soon, your expectations are that nothing will ever improve in your life again. That's a challenging place to be in.

Early in our dream adventure, Tony and I met a great couple on one of our trips. They both had very successful careers and MBAs from Ivy League colleges. The husband had achieved success beyond his dreams during the dot.com era and lost it all at the end of that era. He believed the best of his life was over and he was only 35 years old. He had stopped dreaming about possibilities because he became paralyzed by the problems of his past.

It doesn't have to be that way.

Visualize a teeter-totter. In the center is a fulcrum that creates the teeter-totter's perfect balance. On one side are your expectations—dreams, desires, and vision. On the other side is a box filled with stark reality—your skills, abilities, and capabilities. Equally as important, that box also contains your willingness to do what is necessary to achieve your expectations. The challenge of the teeter-totter comes from creating a balance on both sides to make great things happen. Obstacles are part of the reality that we cannot always foresee in our dreaming and planning stage. Accepting the lessons learned from situations that derail us during our adventure is part of the journey to realizing our dreams.

Remember what it felt like when you graduated from high school and headed toward the life of your dreams? You were now in charge of your choices. You probably had high expectations of what your life was going to be like at the end of four or five years. You dreamt about what type of career and quality of life you were going to have; whether you were going to get married; what kind of family you would have; and even what kind of house you were going to live in. These are huge expectations, and more often than not, nobody explained how much work was involved with making them a reality. Those who choose to further their education may not be aware that 30 percent of college students drop out after their first year, and half of the students who enroll in college don't finish and graduate. It's important to inject a healthy dose of reality into your dreams and be willing to do whatever it takes within your personal limitations to achieve the expectations you set for yourself.

One way to accomplish this is to make a list of your dreams and expectations in all aspects of your life, and then balance it with the reality of what is required to make those dreams come true. Resist falling into the trap of looking at the lives of famous people—athletes, musicians, dancers, actors—and desiring what they have. Instead, look in the mirror, take an inventory and ask yourself: What talents and skills do I have? What do I love to do? When using these skills, does time fly and am I filled with an energy I can't explain? Do others tell me, "Wow, you're really great at that"?

> Take ownership of whatever it is you decide you want out of life because you're the only one that can make it reality.

When you take this self-inventory and stay with your talents and skills, you begin to tap into them to build amazing dreams and create expectations of realistic success. On the other hand, when you're not really good at something but decide to make that your career, you are setting yourself up for disappointment and frustration. Your expectation is high but your skill set and talents don't match the expectation. That must be part of your balancing act. Ask yourself if your expectations include skills and abilities that you're able to learn if you don't already possess them? If so, where can you go to improve?

Consider NBA Hall of Famer Larry Bird. During his playing days, Larry would take more than 300 practice shots each day as part of his pregame conditioning—even though he already had one of the deadliest jump shots in the game. His expectations were set so high that his reality was that he had to strive to achieve nothing less than perfection. Larry had the skill set to attempt this quest. The lesson is simple: Even if you're really great at something, you need to keep working on it to get better. When you set high expectations, in order to achieve your dreams, you must work hard to get there and continuously improve, taking nothing for granted.

I've seen and read about entrepreneurs who decided they wanted to make a lot of money or start a new business because they read an article about somebody who started a new business and was successful. Their logic is that if somebody else is doing it, they should be able to do it, too. That's not a good example to mimic. Too often, we don't have the skills or ability to do the same thing others do and never take the time to do our homework to assess whether that dream could be a good fit. Too many of us just say, "I'm going to do this because she did it." Like it or not, there's a lot of hard work that goes into balancing expectations and reality.

When someone is working in their natural talent and developed skill set it looks easy to everyone watching. Many successful people become inspired by someone else's success, add their own natural talent, and maximize the idea to create their own success story. They weren't interested in merely copying what someone else did—they put their own stamp on their story. A great example is Starbucks. Yes, I enjoy Starbucks frequently and have been inspired by Howard

Schultz's tale of making purchasing a cup of coffee a special event so we will spend more money on "just a cup of coffee"—which, by the way has been around for a very long time! He completely put his trust in his dream. Then used his talents and skills, surrounding himself with people utilizing talents and skills he lacked, to create the success we see today.

People think you can just get lucky if you dream big. Reality is that you create your own luck through hard work and awareness of the delicate balancing act between expectations and reality.

Several years ago I was being interviewed for a magazine article and was asked what the most important things an entrepreneur needs to do in order to be successful. This is a big dream for many and I did not take the question lightly. I explained there are four very basic and important things: Do what you say, finish what you start, show up on time, and always say please and thank you.

The interviewer came back and said, "No, Mary, really, what does somebody have to do to make sure they are successful in business?"

So I replied that she may not have heard me correctly, let me say it differently: "Do what you say, finish what you start, always show up on time, and always say please and thank you."

She said, "I'm not sure you're taking my question seriously."

I admit I did chuckle a little when I replied, "The fact is if you want to achieve anything or have any kind of expectation, you have to do what you say you're going to do. You must finish whatever it is that you start. If you tell somebody you're going to do something, you have to do it. If you tell somebody you're going to be there at a certain time or if you own a business and you say you're going to open at 9 o'clock, that business should be open at 9 o'clock. Finally, always be grateful and gracious to others."

My point was that you have to set realistic expectations about what's required to be successful. Some of the action steps may feel unimportant, but you need to take into consideration that you need others to fulfill your dreams. If you don't consider the impact your actions have on others you are setting yourself up for disappointment. You don't need to be the highest educated or richest person in the room, or the best at any one thing. If you identify your skills and talents, consider the impact your behavior has on the result, and set realistic expectations, you can dream big—about almost anything. When you work hard using those skills and talents, you can make your dreams come true. By the end of our conversation she was surprised that my philosophy was so straightforward and simple.

At JANCOA, for example, we learned a hard lesson about balancing expectations with reality when we started taking a hard look at our business model and customer base. As entrepreneurs, we don't like to say "No" to any prospective client. Who wants to turn away business? Not every customer should be your customer—and that's a very hard thing to accept. We clean large buildings very well. That's what we do. When we focus on attracting this type of business and gaining customers who appreciate our talents and capabilities, JANCOA thrives and grows. We exceed expectations. We have a 45-year history and experience to know what works and doesn't work for our business, customers, and employees. When we were hustling business to land clients regardless of the type of buildings and the prospects and customers did not ask or care about our employees we did not have the success we wanted to achieve. No one wins in a situation where you try to be the jack-of-all-trades and master of none—where you spend the entire day trying to make everyone happy by saying "Yes" and not living by the principles and standards you find important. This is something that was crystallized when a competitor gave me one of the best compliments I ever received. He said, "Mary, I can always tell a JANCOA building by the restrooms and the lobbies."

The bottom line is that today we know what we do best and have grown by staying close to our core. We recognized that we couldn't be people pleasers when it undermines our quality and values as an organization and individuals to meet a client's demands. However, by knowing and being true to ourselves and having the courage to say no to a request that we know from our experience would be costly and not achieve the desired result, then we can please people through exceptional service and keeping the promises we make. We stay focused on balancing expectations and reality while staying true to our principles. We have become a resource to our clients by helping them realize the best way to achieve the results they strive to have.

Another example relates to the way we deal with the obstacles preventing us from achieving our results. Tony and I were working on our employee turnover rate, which had become a very serious issue. The average turnover in our industry is estimated at 360 to 400 percent. We were hiring 50 people every month. We were conducting background tests, drug screenings, and training each new employee. It was expensive to hire and lose so many people each month. Despite our efforts, we were still at least 30 people short every night. This put a great deal of stress on those people who showed up to work each shift. The overtime was an additional expense and our best people were worn out. Our long-term employees knew that no matter what, the customers could not notice the problem we were having. Many times, you could find Tony and I working day and night to make sure everything was taken care of for the customers. Delivering our promises to the customers was the highest priority.

Do you set realistic expectations for yourself based on your personal skills and talent?

We had a dilemma: What were we going to do? We had even hired a consultant who fired us the second day of a weeklong contract! He told us that we had to fix our people problem; not having enough people everyday had become unacceptable and even though that was the industry average we decided not to be average any longer. We had big dreams for our business and the reality was that our dream wasn't looking good at that time.

Initially, Tony thought we needed to start hiring 70 people every month in an effort to increase our personnel numbers so that we would have a better chance of more people staying with the company. It's simple math, but expensive math that doesn't address the people problem.

I was struggling with this option, but up until this moment I wasn't sure what the solution was. I believed this option wasn't going to work. We needed a new strategy, something more pragmatic. We needed to shift our thinking and face this problem with a different perspective. We were not seeing the sunrise. There was nothing sunny about our problematic attrition rate.

"We can't just keep bringing in more employees every month—our people problem is not going away by hiring more workers if we don't make some real changes around here and look at the situation from a different angle," I said.

That got Tony's attention. He wasn't used to me coming from a different direction and seeing things that differently. I was using my talent and acquired skills in our industry to examine the situation. My voice was also beginning to find its way.

"So what are you recommending?" he asked.

"First, we need to stop this revolving door and focus on what it takes to attract the best people who want to work in our industry to work for JANCOA," I said. "This isn't about bringing in more people. It's about bringing in the right people."

We needed to ask different questions—the ones we were asking weren't getting us anywhere. Instead of playing a numbers game of bringing in 70 people each month in an attempt to keep enough workers to fill the schedule, we needed to ask probing questions about the future:

- What will make JANCOA an employer of choice for our industry in our community?
- What training do they need to be successful?
- How can we get them to want to stay working at JANCOA?
- What would that environment look like and how would it differentiate us from competitors?

By asking different questions, we got different answers. This changed the way we saw our dreams and expectations, and we began to align our dreams of an engaged and loyal workforce with our expectations and reality of the people we employed. Most significantly, our Dream Manager program emerged from this bold, new attitude, and we began offering programs for employees to create value for them. We looked into their quality of life and asked them what they wanted. We listened to their words and watched their actions. We filtered our skills and abilities into the Dream Manager program so our people could reach their goals to improve their quality of life: getting drivers' licenses, taking English classes, buying homes or cars, providing opportunities for their children. We were empowered to change direction with the belief that by doing better for our people, we would all feel more fulfilled in our lives. It was a big dream, a huge expectation, but completely balanced with the reality of what we could accomplish.

The first step was taking ownership. That's a powerful lesson: Whatever it is you decide you want to do in life, own it. This is different than making a list or a statement about the dream you want in your life and just sitting back and waiting for it to happen TO you. Taking ownership means you proclaim what you want and are willing to DO what it takes to achieve your dream. Success of any type doesn't happen to those who wait for it to come to them. Dreaming is a verb, an action that you need to own and be willing to carry out.

Start with a list of dreams you want to do, be, and achieve. There are all kinds of dreams in life and it doesn't start or end with buying something material. That is one kind of dream. Try this exercise to give yourself clarity about your future. Start with a clean notebook and write on the front: "MY FUTURE STARTS NOW." Start with a blank page, set a timer for five minutes, and start writing all the dreams you would like to happen in your lifetime. Let your mind go wild and write everything that comes to mind without analyzing or rationalizing. Include all aspects of your life: personal, professional, financial, health, relationships. My hope is that your list brings a lot of excitement and maybe a little fear; the blend of both creates an energy that will move you into action. The next step is to review the list and circle the top three items you want to work on in the next year. YOU determine

Set realistic expectations for the work necessary to make your business successful. Be sure to consider the impact your actions have on others.

the priorities for YOUR life. Create an action plan and time frame on each of the items, this will start the momentum to achieve those dreams. Use the energy created to take the first step in that direction. List these top three on a separate page and create a column next to it listing how you will feel when you have achieved each dream on your list and another column listing one action to move the momentum forward.

Maybe one dream is a new job that really excites you and adds energy to your life just thinking about the possibilities. What does that look like? Now, write a story focused on looking back one year from now. What does your life look like (as if it's already happened) using the list you made from the exercise in the previous paragraph? Let's say you love jewelry and want to own a jewelry store.

- What does that look like for your life?
- What information do you need to know and what are you willing to do to make that happen?
- What are the expectations you're setting for yourself as part of that dream?
- Is it that you want to earn more money or would love to be in a management position?
- Do you want to be a business owner so that you have more time doing what you love to do? Or maybe you want to have more time with your family?
- Is your dream that you want to have better benefits? Or maybe you want to offer your own employees better benefits so that they have a better life?
- Do you want to have time to develop your professional career? Or would you like to be able to offer people promotions and help them build their career?

It is important that you ask yourself a lot of questions as you create your dream list of the future. Dig down deeper than what you see on the surface. Have conversations with others who have excelled in the areas important to you. Own it and be aware of what you have to do to make your expectations a reality.

Once you determine your top three to five priorities for the year, determine all those things you want to achieve as part of that dream and expectation. Make those the focus of your action list. Always remember there is not a bad goal moving toward your dreams, you have to adjust the timing sometimes and gain new capabilities to achieve them. Your talents should always be part of the activities needed to make the dream a reality. The bottom line is that you want to be able to see the expectation, but not just in your head. As long as you keep your thoughts in your head, your imagination will distort reality and frequently feed you with negative self-talk, adding fear and anxiety to your life. You have to get it out of your head and put it on paper so you can see it and then begin to visualize it happening. When you see it on paper it makes your dreams and possibilities real, and you can start doing things to move in the direction of your dreams.

Looking at your list, put one of the dreams on a separate page. This is your reality check. Figure out some of the obstacles that might be a barrier to achieving your expectations and make a list under the dream. These should be items that you don't feel you can get around—even if you get lucky. One possible obstacle could be that you don't have the

> Expectations are what you want to have in your life; reality is knowing and using your skills and talent to achieve what's important to you.

qualifications necessary, so you may have great (or perceived great) difficulty trying to achieve that specific dream. Maybe you lack strong references or connections. Perhaps you need more money to cover startup costs. Or don't know enough about the industry you're hoping to enter. Start making a list of all the different obstacles that could get in the way. Next, create a column next to the obstacles and list strategies one at a time for each obstacle. Clear action steps will surface that you can take now to help you balance expectations with reality.

I heard a story once about a young person who went to a McDonald's with his grandfather. The grandfather looked at him while he was eating his burger and fries and said, "You know, there are three different choices people can make. There are people who make somebody else's hamburger. There are people who manage somebody's hamburger store. Then there is the person who owns the hamburger store. It's all up to you to decide. What are you going to be?" Our future starts with the way we choose to look at opportunities and the actions we are willing to take to make them reality. It's not about good, bad, right, or wrong at this point. When I was younger, I never considered owning a business as an option. It really can be as simple as choosing and doing what needs to happen to achieve the dreams you want.

There are different ways you can look at what you want to do in life, whether you're building your home, career, or business. We all have dreams. There is expectation and there is reality, and they have to be balanced. We frequently make life more complicated than it needs to be. Keep your actions as simple as possible, align to help people you trust, and enjoy achieving the reality of your dreams.

CHAPTER 4
Eliminate Obstacles

"If you always do what you've always done,
you'll always get what you've always got."
—Henry Ford

Successful people share a common trait: When faced with a seemingly insurmountable challenge, they don't stop at the wall that blocks their way; they find a way past it. Each solution may be different—it could take them around the wall, over it, under it, or even right through it—but in every case the obstacles are something to eliminate rather than tolerate or avoid because they stand in the way of progress. The focus is on the solution rather than being stuck in the problem.

Often, what gets in the way for many of us is a misguided belief that if you work hard you'll be successful. Unfortunately, no matter how hard you work, obstacles pop up to block your path. It's what you do next—how you get past the wall—that defines you and leads to success.

So how can you transform challenges and obstacles into opportunities?

Change your direction from how you are viewing the situation—from working hard to working smart—and analyze what you're doing so that you can ask the question, "Why?"

You may not like the answers you discover, but if you accept them as fact you'll better understand the obstacle and be able to identify solutions that obliterate the wall and set you back on your way toward achieving your dreams.

Here's an example: Most people hear a lion's roar and instantly associate it with danger. What they don't realize is that as lions age their roar becomes louder. It's a ploy lions use to trap prey. Older lions are the ones who roar loudly so that the game they are hunting run away from the roar. Waiting for them are the younger, faster lions, with sharper teeth and claws. When it comes to obstacles, you don't want to run away from the roar; you want to run toward it. That's where the opportunities exist. You just need the courage to confront them.

During JANCOA's darkest moments we faced serious problems that stood in the way of our success. It wasn't until we decided to charge directly toward the loud roar that we discovered our greatest opportunities. Obstacles are an important part of life. Don't fear them, and don't avoid them. Use your life experiences to uncover a solution and then rely upon your innate talents and skills to pursue it.

Admittedly, not everybody has the skill, talent, or know-how to overcome every obstacle they face. You might need to recruit help to apply whatever solution you land upon. That's why it is so important to develop your instincts and knowledge base so that you can realize what you're capable of doing—and what you're not. For example, I'm not an IT person. I could never be Steve Jobs or Bill Gates. They recognized their talents and limitations, then went out and created new opportunities in their industry. They surrounded themselves with others who had skills they lacked, and together they realized the future each envisioned. You can do the same by eliminating the obstacles that stand in the way of achieving your dreams.

For Tony and me, it was realizing that playing the numbers game and hiring more people to fill in when employees inevitably left us was not the right answer. The mere thought of finding nearly 100 new recruits every month was overwhelming because when a business has to hire in high volume like we were doing, you are more concerned with filling holes than finding the right people to fill roles. There's a remarkable difference between those two things, and quality suffers when your mindset shifts to quantity. It was getting to the point where we had to go from asking, "Who can we get this week?" to "How can we keep who we have?"

JANCOA had become an industry average business with a revolving door and our sustainability as an organization was dependent on finding the right solution. We had tried a consultant, but that approach failed. After he fired us, we recognized it was up to us. Neither Tony nor I knew what the right fix was. We understood we needed a completely different approach, so we began looking for better answers than we had. It started with changing the questions we were asking. Instead of focusing on the questions: Why were our employees leaving us? What was preventing them from showing up on time to work? Why were they calling in sick? We focused on questions to lead us to the result we wanted to accomplish: What would attract employees to work for us? What training do they need to be successful? How can we get them to want to stay at JANCOA? What environment will differentiate us from the competition?

Finally, Tony and I determined the best question to start our new standard: What did our best people have in common? We started paying closer attention to issues that we had previously accepted as normal business situations for our industry.

We opened our ears and listened closely to what the employees were telling us—albeit through nonverbal cues. By doing so, we learned that the problem was something so simple that it was right in front of us the entire time: transportation.

Many of our workers did not speak English, they did not have drivers' licenses, and they relied on public transportation. In our community, public transportation doesn't reach the neighborhoods where our employees lived. Even more problematic, public transportation doesn't run on the hours our employees need it to run. While our shifts run all hours, we clean most buildings at night when cubicles are quiet and employees are gone. Our standard shift begins at 6 p.m. and finishes at 2:30 a.m. These were serious obstacles preventing our employees and JANCOA from moving forward. We believed that by solving the challenge of our employees getting to JANCOA, we could alleviate a significant stress for our workers.

So Monday morning Tony bought a 15-passenger van. He took it to a sign-painting store and had a JANCOA logo painted on the side with the words "JANCOA Employee Shuttle." Tony pulled the van up to the office, ready to start transporting our people to work, and back home after work. There was one more obstacle we hadn't thought about: We didn't have anybody to drive the van. We were short on people to clean the buildings we were contracted to clean, let alone drive a shuttle around. So in true entrepreneurial spirit, Tony became our first shuttle driver.

For the first two weeks, Tony drove the shuttle all over the city. Within two days, he was invisible—employees didn't even realize the owner of the business was driving them around. This became another opportunity for us: Being invisible led us to a whole new capability that we didn't know existed because we could hear the conversations our employees were having with each other. We heard problems they were having that they had not shared with us before. Further, because we were picking them up at home, we saw the conditions in which they were living. These factors, combined, made such a huge difference in our approach to solving our people problem because suddenly we could see that there were different things going on in our employees' lives that we had not previously considered. We were in a position to actually do something about it.

That van became the ultimate focus group. We continued to listen to our people. As we did, Tony and I realized that our people problem would only be remedied with some innovative problem-solving. We decided to look deeper than the turnover stats and focus on cultural change. From there, we thought that employee retention would rise. As it turned out, there were many other roadblocks JANCOA's employees faced and goals they wanted to reach: Learning to speak English. Buying a home. Getting a driver's license. Purchasing a car. Taking classes to improve skill sets. Setting an example for their children so they could build a better future.

With this newfound insight, everything suddenly shifted. JANCOA could be so much more than a janitorial services company if we could find a way to help our people focus on improving their quality of life and creating a bigger future doing what they wanted. A good friend said to us one day "You are really helping your team dream about their future." That really clicked with us and we realized that if we changed our focus to helping them dream about what they wanted—and become a company with a mission to serve our team members (they just happened to be janitors)—we could make a significant difference in their lives, impact the community, and JANCOA's problems would also be reduced. It was a win-win situation.

> Obstacles are an important part of life so don't fear them or avoid them. Instead, use your life experiences to uncover solutions and then rely on your unique talents to achieve them.

It's funny, when you use your skills and abilities to create value for people, whether in their personal or business lives, their lives change and your life changes as well. When people achieve their dreams, their lives improve and they get excited. The more excited they get, the more motivated they become to help others have the same opportunity for change that they have. It is a ripple effect. So, our obstacle transformed into an opportunity. By embracing change, Tony and I recognized there was no way we could grow JANCOA and eliminate the problems the business faced if we kept doing "the usual." The more we got to know our employees, the more I recognized they wanted the same things out of life that we did—secure jobs that provided meaning for their lives and created a legacy for their children and grandchildren to achieve their own dreams.

This was transformational and completely changed the way we did things. Instead of focusing on turnover, and the cost associated with it, we focused on retention and improving the lives of our "JANCOA Family." Yes, we changed the way we started looking at our employees. Now they became team members and part of the "JANCOA Family."

As the process continued, Tony would come home from driving our employee shuttle and say, "Man, these people have problems. They have problems I didn't even know existed. They've got 12 people living in a two-bedroom apartment. They've got children that can't get up and go to school in the morning because the parents are just getting home from work and can't get up."

The two of us put our heads together and began to think of new ideas, new solutions to leverage JANCOA to help make a difference in their lives. We began talking to different agencies around Cincinnati, asking questions about how they worked with people to finance homes, pursue an education, and learn about personal finances. As we did this, and without realizing what was happening, we talked to more and more people quietly building a network of connections that could be leveraged later. We were fixated on finding ways to help our people. Somewhere along the way, Tony and I changed—our hearts starting opening up in ways we had never thought about, and what was originally a process change suddenly turned into a humanity change. Instead of just focusing on a process that needed people pushing brooms or running vacuum cleaners, we start thinking of our people as people and connecting with their individual and collective problems on a more human level. This made all the difference in the world. Obstacles started melting away like an iceberg into the ocean—slowly but visible.

We connected with organizations like the Home Ownership Center and learned they had numerous programs to help first time homebuyers. A lot of our people were first generation homeowners, no one in their families had ever owned a home. So, we started helping people buy homes and change their thinking about future possibilities. They could start to visualize much brighter futures.

We celebrated with our team members. We brought cakes and balloons to celebrate at their closings. The title agency staff would look at us like we were crazy.

"It's just signing paperwork," one told us. "We do this all day long."

"You don't understand," I said. "Nobody in this family had ever bought—or owned—a home before. This is special."

In addition, we helped families refinance their homes to reduce their debt. We connected them with agencies to learn budgeting and financial literacy so that they could plan for their families to budget ahead of time rather than living paycheck to paycheck. This allowed their children to dream and make plans to go to college. For other people, we helped them learn to speak English so they could improve their quality of life. We helped employees who had never completed high school earn their GEDs to access greater employment opportunities, and move on to bigger and better jobs than we had to offer. Some of those people went on to complete other studies, such as nursing school. There are dozens of wonderful success stories over the years.

Our initiative changed names a few times. It started as the "Incredible Employee Retention" program, and then became "The Dream Engineer" but we soon changed it to the "Dream Manager" program when Matthew Kelly wrote a book inspired by what we had created.

The name was designed to get our team members and their families excited about the future. We wanted them to see it was possible to overcome the obstacles in their lives and to change what they didn't know; to stop going through the motions of survival and to transform it into opportunity and hope that tomorrow could be drastically different than yesterday.

We hired a full-time Dream Manager to manage the program for the team members and an executive director to manage the business. Our thinking was that the Dream Manager would help people dream while our existing HR managers would work on traditional compliance issues. These were two very different roles within our company.

Our Dream Manager started hosting group sessions on Saturday mornings. He would sit down with eight to 10, and even sometimes 15 people. They talked about their dreams and encouraged each other to fulfill them. During one of my favorite sessions

> **If you don't turn around and face the right direction you'll never see the rising sun.**

we supplied magazines to a large gym of team members and families who wanted to dream. They each were given a board so they could create their own Dream Board. There were team members that had never spoken to me because of their concern that their English wasn't good enough and they told me all about their dreams of the future. It was an amazing event.

Early on, an employee's wife called the office.

"My husband doesn't want to go to those sessions on Saturday," she said, "but I want to buy a house. Can I come?"

We decided to open the Dream Manager program to the families of our team members. Why not? It was designed to help our people—and that included their families.

This outstanding culture of connectedness created a whole new energy. The problem that we initially had getting people to come to work was gone. Our solution-focused programs completely altered the company. Now our employees were helping us solve our people problem by bringing new people in to join the JANCOA Family and mission. The shuttle was the first step that reduced our turnover to a manageable percentage, but it was the Dream Manager program that led to people coming through our doors. The ripple effect of the energy it infused our team members with was staggering—and it didn't take long before our own obstacles to growth were greatly reduced. Instead of being 38 full-time people short every day we now had enough employees to get the job accomplished and grow. People were calling, wanting jobs that we didn't have openings for, causing a huge shift in the whole culture of our business.

Eventually, our customers noticed that they were seeing the same people every day. They wanted to know what we were doing right with our team members. They wanted to learn about this Dream Manager program we established. We even had a few customers attend the Saturday sessions and one purchased a home through the program.

When I started to work at JANCOA with Tony, my own personal obstacles were coming into focus. I had not yet fully embraced my role as Tony's co-conspirator in the business, but was seeing all this positive energy around me. Finally, he said, "You have to stop thinking like an employee and start thinking like a business owner."

"What does that mean?" I asked.

"You have to trust your instincts. Sometimes, it's easier to ask for forgiveness than permission."

That became my "Go" pass, it was life changing and I started to trust myself more—not just when dealing with the business, but life as a whole. It was permission—encouragement really—to let go of my longstanding habits that had up until that point stood in the way of allowing me to make strong but possibly risky business decisions.

I started thinking about the long-term future of JANCOA. I began to examine all the obstacles standing in our way. Sure, we had improved our people problem, but for JANCOA that really meant we had achieved nothing more than temporary, short-term results. It didn't address the other issues hindering our ability to grow.

One problem was that up until then, I didn't have enough information to make the tough decisions that needed to be made. Tony's encouraging words unleashed something within me, an ability to eliminate a personnel obstacle I was reluctant to face. Now I was ready to make the tough calls that would help us unlock JANCOA's potential. With our personnel issue improving, something still didn't seem quite right. I was optimistic that positive change was out there for the first time—like the new day's sun on the horizon. I dug in and began examining every nook and cranny of the company, seeking new ways to improve what we were doing. I read everything I could get my hands on about business. I attended seminars. I listened to and picked the brains of other business people. Little by little I began to notice patterns, some that worked and some that didn't.

One of the big issues I realized needed attention was our relationship with one of our largest clients, which was not sustainable over the long run. This was the client we dropped everything for and ran to please— the one that was named first when someone asked, "Who are your customers?"

Without naming names, at the time we brought in a large check each month from a business that occupied class A office space. Cleaning their toilets was considered a privilege, at least we had always thought of it that way. For over a decade, this prestigious client was the headliner on our "it" list, and we allowed their satisfaction to define our worth. However, as I had painfully learned earlier in my life, people pleasing doesn't work well in the long term. Whenever you work painstakingly hard to please others, you are working without direction. It's like getting behind the wheel and driving on the open road without stopping for fuel, a rest break, or checking your route. You just drive. You're on automatic pilot, running full speed ahead. After a while, you realize that you missed every single road sign and a lot of interesting stops along the way. You never reach your end point because there is no defined destination, and you just run out of gas. If life is all about the journey, this is no way to travel.

Like these kind of blind journeys, to rectify your situation you have to pull over, re-evaluate your course, and possibly even question the route you chose. Do you turn here to go a different direction? Should you backtrack a bit to find a better road? For JANCOA, this destination-less journey required us to face a difficult reality—and consider making a very tough decision. With Tony handling everything himself, he didn't necessarily have the ability to stop, pull over, and re-evaluate things. Now he had me to help handle things he didn't previously have time for.

> To overcome obstacles, recognize your talent limitations—what you're capable of doing and what you're not—and surround yourself with others who have the skills you lack. Build your tribe!

It turned out we spent years not making a decent profit and scrambling to please this client, which only cared about its bottom line. In taking stock of our client base, I took a hard look at every one of them and asked myself what was working and what wasn't. I came to the conclusion that people pleasing compromised our integrity as an organization. Further, we needed to give ourselves permission to act on our intuition and talent, to do what we knew was best for our company. That's never easy. I was the person who could stop the car and say, "Wait a minute. You're going the wrong way. Pull over and get out a map."

We had to do a brake check for JANCOA—we were doing it for our employees and now it was time to do it for ourselves. Life and business don't work well when you only focus on making other people happy. In the case of this significant client, the relationship was not thriving no matter how hard we worked. We felt stuck. They were a huge percentage of our annual business, which is why we had never questioned whether we should be on the job. In looking at our numbers I was struck that we simply were not making money on this large-volume account. Plus, it was draining our people. We had to scramble to fill positions because the turnover of the people servicing the account was so high. It was time to step up and make a tough decision. We had to change direction.

After double and triple checking our numbers, and then raking through our client list, I made my first bold move. I was pretty sure Tony was not going to like the news.

"I know how we can save more than $1,000 every month," I told him. "I know how we can make more money, improve our employee retention, and get more business."

This was not a sales pitch. This was a game changer for JANCOA.

He was curious, amused. "How?"

"We need to fire this prized customer."

Huh? The look on his face said, "Mary, you've lost your mind. I love you, and you're crazy."

I was serious. I knew I was right. I trusted myself.

"We have lost more than $100,000 serving that customer over the past ten years," I said. Like it or not, our top client was killing us. Either they had to pay us more, or we needed to trade the time spent servicing their account on generating new sales that would produce a better profit and foster a set-up-to-succeed environment for our people. Besides, with the Dream Manager program in play and our efforts to jump-start a better environment for our workers underway, we were not setting the right example by keeping a client that was an energy drain on our people. Sticking with this customer under our then contract was facing west while trying to see the sunrise. You've got to spend time with people who have their batteries included, not people who drain your energy. The same goes for clients.

"We have to ask them for a raise, or fire this client right now," I told Tony.

My findings did not please him. They didn't please me either, to be honest. Who wants to crunch the numbers and find out their hero account is, in fact, the albatross of the customer roster?

"So, what are you proposing?" Tony asked.

"Well, I think we need to be straightforward with them and tell them that we need a raise, otherwise we can't afford to continue doing business with them. If they value the relationship, they'll understand and respect our proposal. If they don't, well…"

"What if they don't?" Tony pressed. "How can we afford to lose them?"

"How can we afford to keep them?" I asked.

The numbers told the story that neither of us wanted to acknowledge. This was definitely a pit stop we didn't plan on in our journey. It was a big obstacle. The more we looked deeply inside the organization and began asking tough questions, the more we realized we were not always going to get the answers we wanted. The easy ones, that is. It's tough to change. It's painful to look in another direction sometimes, because you're afraid of what you'll see and how it will affect your life or business. You think, "Why can't we just keep humming along? We're all happy. No one's getting hurt here." If you continue walking with blinders on, you'll miss the peripheral view. If you don't turn around and face the right direction, you won't see the rising sun—the new opportunity revealing itself. You'll miss the answer—the aha!—the reason you're here. You will never overcome the obstacles standing in the way of your happiness and success. This is the first step to realizing your purpose and potential in life.

Tony and I understood all of this, yet we were afraid to confront a client that represented a large percentage of our overall business. We either needed to increase our price to serve them or basically ask for our own pink slip. What about our people? What about our bottom line? Would we completely fail as a business?

I had a gut instinct on this one, along with the numbers to back it up. The numbers were showing us what we didn't want to see—our best client was toxic for our organization. That's a hard reality to face. And acting on that truth is even more difficult, but we had no choice. We could not correct our turnover problem if we kept servicing this client the way we were.

I quoted Henry Ford at the open of this chapter, and many others have reaffirmed it since, "If you always do what you've always done, you'll always get what you've always got." It was time for us to get paid more or get out. Our business, and our people, deserved to be treated fairly. While this was a major business risk, the benefit of losing the account (and the money) justified asking for a raise. We were losing money on this client. Our team was overworked and unfulfilled because they were tasked with a job that they could not possibly complete with success. The client was focused on price, and we were accommodating that demand at the expense of our own profit and our people's happiness.

Oh, we talked this one to death before going to the client. Tony trusted me with all his heart—he always does. That's the way a solid partnership works. You've got to believe in yourself and let that belief guide you when times get tough.

Tony picked up the phone and scheduled a meeting with the client. He had been working with them for several years and had a strong relationship. He had a conversation with them that included the obstacle we were facing and asked the customer for the raise. I explained the numbers and set out our case. I focused on the long relationship JANCOA had with them and our desire to continue that rapport and enrich it by taking it to a higher level. That would mean being compensated fairly for the work performed so we could fulfill our promise to our staff to offer a rewarding, beneficial work environment where they can succeed and prosper. We wanted to be fair for both them and us. It was about time, according to the numbers.

The client replied, "We're going to go out to bid then. I suggest that you sharpen your pencil." Seriously! He expected us to lower the price. This was not a win-win situation. So be it. We lost our biggest account and we asked for it. We knew going in that the only way to get to a positive outcome was that there had to be a change. Leaving things as they were was the only negative outcome.

Losing this client and the terms we were working under was a tremendous gain for our business. Really, it was the best thing that could have happened for us—a real turning point for JANCOA. We took a good, hard look at our client list and some of the customers that were spending less for our services; they ended up being our strongest relationships and they were profitable clients. Once we figured the total cost of executing each job, we began developing a list of prospective customers we would like to have—and ones we should not keep or pursue. We had a profitable path to follow—we found our sweet spot focused on a win-win formula.

I've heard somewhere that without obstacles in life, you never have an opportunity, and I know the most difficult obstacles I've ever gone through always led me to better things. If I hadn't gone through two divorces, I would have never met my husband of almost 25 years. If the consultant hadn't fired us, we would never have started the Dream Manager program and started focusing on our team members. That action led us on a journey that made us take a deep look at what we really needed to do to resolve our people problem. That, in turn, led us to review our client roster and make tough decisions that improved our business and our lives. I sometimes feel like Alice in Wonderland balancing both sides of the mirror, two sides of reality.

During the course of one year, our turnover rate fell from 400 to 224 percent. We posted a record profit that year (which means we finally made a profit!), and reduced our absenteeism by 31 percent. Our team member tardiness was reduced by 45 percent. After we took the big step of firing our biggest client, JANCOA integrated the lessons learned from overcoming obstacles and focused on the humanity and relationship components of our team members and customers. Today, JANCOA has a retention of customers and employees that makes our competitors envious. They ask our vendors: "How does JANCOA do it?"

In life, too often when obstacles show up, it stops us in our tracks and it just defeats people. When you see an obstacle as something that is going to help you grow, you change direction. We don't go to see movies about people who never achieved their dreams. We go see movies about people who achieved their dreams after they were almost defeated. We want to see the heroes and hear their extraordinary stories. How did

> Knowing which direction to face must be a conscious and deliberate decision that you're willing to follow through on to the end.

they do it? Diamonds don't just come out of a coal mine. They come out of years of pressure that turns an ugly piece of coal into a beautiful diamond. We all have pressure. We all face obstacles. You can create your own energy—and strength to press on. Energy doesn't come from an exterior source. It comes from within us. It starts by achievements and wells up when awareness about yourself awakens. Then, amazing things can happen. Once you stop listening to the naysayers and your inner critical voice, you can begin to view the obstacles in your life as nothing more than opportunities, and with creative solutions change will happen.

I love the definition of initiative: The ability to solve problems and take actions by thinking of the solutions rather than being told or ordered what to do. When we choose to take initiative, all of the obstacles around us become opportunities to achieve greater things in life. It's a magical thing. Walt Disney is one of my favorite examples and mentors. When you visit the magical kingdom of Disney World you can feel the power of possibility and dreams that have been achieved. Reading his history you can see clearly the obstacles he faced to make that magic happen. It wasn't by sitting at a desk wishing for things to be different. It's taking the difficult steps to acknowledge the obstacles, listing strategies to overcome each obstacle, and doing the work necessary to achieve your dreams. Being grateful for each obstacle allows you to move forward to the results you want in your life.

CHAPTER 5
Create Meaningful Dialogue and Relationships

"Miracles start to happen when you give as much energy
to your dreams as you do to your fears."
—Richard Wilkins

How often have you had a conversation with someone who didn't really care about what it was the two of you were talking about? Maybe you were walking down the hallway, ran into a colleague and said, "How are you today?" Did either of you take the time to stop and engage with each other, or did you both just nod your heads, utter "Good," and go your separate ways? If you stopped, did you take the time to look the other person in the eye and actually listen to their response?

While you can't stop to converse with everyone you pass in the hallway, you can make a conscious effort to have a conversation with him or her at a more convenient time. It's important to make time to build rapport and camaraderie with the people in your life. Positive Focus is a great way to open the lines of communication.

It's easy to tell when someone cares about a conversation or if it's just an act. Meaningful dialogue is powerful. It creates connections. Creating meaningful dialogue with others starts with active listening—acknowledging what the other person said. This doesn't mean repeating word-for-word what they uttered, but rather saying it in a way that demonstrates you were listening and understood what they meant. It's a subtle difference, but active listening is one of the best ways you can show care and respect. When you create meaningful dialogue, you connect immediately, and when you create connections you build trust. Trust is the foundation for relationships where people truly care about one another—whether in business or one's personal life.

For years, I've made it a point to remember something personal about every person I interact with. That may sound difficult, but I learned how to do this years ago when I was in sales. It's called my tickler file, and when I run into someone I start the conversation around a fact gleaned from a previous conversation. For example, I might ask, "How is Joey doing on his baseball team? Did he enjoy his last season?" The person I'm speaking with will be stunned that I remembered that they had a son, let alone that his name is Joey and that he plays baseball. This simple gesture demonstrates that I not only remembered our last conversation, but listened to what they said. It shows respect and creates a sense of connection. It says, "I care about you."

Today more than ever, people can tell if you're faking it. When you keep walking as you mutter, "How are you?" you fall woefully short of making connections. When you stop, look someone in the eye, and concentrate on what they're saying, you acknowledge their humanity. Too often, we're distracted by what we're doing and whatever device we're toting around to care about anyone else. I'm a huge fan of technology and how easy it has made our lives, but we're missing something if we're just communicating via email and text. Just look around you. Are people having real conversations with each other or are they just going through the motions? How can you change direction to create meaningful dialogue and build relationships?

First, make the decision that this change is important to you. Choosing to change your behavior needs to be an active choice. After you decide this is important to you and what results you want to achieve in your relationships you have to make it a habit. This makes it something you go out of your way to do. Review your actions at the end of the day and ask yourself: "How did I do with showing people I cared by the way I listened and paid attention to them?" It must become part of the fabric of your being. Once you make it a habit, you can build upon it. Try this exercise: The next time you're at dinner with family or friends, you can be at home or at a restaurant, ask the people at your table about the best thing that happened to them that day. Take turns talking—and pay attention to what each person says. Why was this "best thing" interesting? What made it so good? Who else was involved?

Engage each other by asking deeper questions about the "best thing," and build off each answer. Then, after everyone has become part of the conversation, ask what everyone is looking forward to about tomorrow.

By having a real conversation that includes asking questions, listening, and acknowledging what you have heard, you will get to know each other that much better. By using active listening, you'll discover things you may not have known. You will develop stronger relationships with friends and family, and you'll add meaning to the words.

In our family, it's a tradition during holidays like Thanksgiving to have thoughtful conversations when we get together because we don't often get to see some of the people involved. We talk about one thing we're grateful for, and then discuss each of those things as a group. What happens is that these build up until we're having a full conversation about what happened to each of us over the past year. Sometimes, these are funny stories. Sometimes, they're more serious. We've even had competitions to see who has the funniest story of the year.

At JANCOA, our Dream Manager focuses on having meaningful conversations as part of the job. We don't just make a list of the employee's dreams. Instead, it's important to take the time to listen and care about what it is the employee is saying. By looking the other person in the eye and asking, "What is it that you really want?" a bond is forged between the two.

Listening means having both ears wide open, as well as having an open heart. When you pay attention to body language you will better understand what they are saying. Learn how to listen without thinking about how you're going to respond when the other person finishes talking. Too often, we're waiting for our moment to talk and not giving the other person our complete attention. The entire tone of the conversation changes when you become an active listener. Instead of answering with what you've been thinking about saying, acknowledge what you heard: "So Tony, if I heard you correctly, you're saying you really want to go on vacation this summer to Miami and spend a week on the beach and not have to do anything."

"Yes," Tony would say. "That would be nice." This type of response in active listening also clears up and clarifies to avoid assumptions.

How often have you had that kind of conversation with anybody in your life? How often has your spouse had that conversation with you? Probably less often than you'd like to admit. Relationships deepen when you develop meaningful dialogue. A typical question I'll ask someone who I don't see very often is "Tell me what's going on in your life that you're really excited about?" That is a great conversation starter because it's positive and allows them to talk about anything they want to discuss—whether it's work-related or personal. Frequently, their passion will show up in the conversation, which also deepens your connection. Taking time to ask and listen is the greatest way to show respect to someone.

A few years ago, at a business event, I struck up a conversation with a woman I didn't know very well. We were learning about each other and I asked her that question. She started telling me what she was excited about—a big birthday that was coming up and a major home renovation. If I hadn't asked, she might have been more guarded and only mentioned, "Work is busy" or "My children are home for the holidays." I would never have learned details about her life and created a connection that didn't exist previously. By asking an open-ended, specific question about her future, I got to know her better and it took our new relationship to a different level.

There is little doubt that relationships can be powerful. In all the speaking and coaching I've done over the past 15 years, nobody has been able to bring me a story about someone on their deathbed who said, "I wish I had more time alone" or "I wish I worked harder or longer." Everybody always says they wish they spent more time with their family or friends. It's in our nature to crave relationships. They are what make us who we are, but relationships don't miraculously happen overnight. They must be intentional—especially your most important relationships.

So why have today's conversations seemingly devolved into meaningless banter? Why are many of us just walking through life in our own worlds—consumed by our various

> Active listening shows others you respect them. By creating meaningful dialogue you build trust, which is the foundation of any valuable relationship.

devices? Focusing too much energy on how many "likes" you get from people that you don't even know or rarely see! Unfortunately, it often comes down to blind spots. We're not cognizant that we're not having meaningful conversations or building relationships with others. We are either too busy or distracted to notice. It doesn't have to be this way. We can change our behavior. We always have a choice.

Make a list of the five most important people in your life. Which one do you want to focus on first? Make a concerted effort to connect with that person, and when you do, instead of trying to show him or her how smart and how great you are, keep the conversation focused on them. How many of these types of conversations can you have in the next 30 days? Start practicing now so they become so natural you don't have to think about it. That is what a habit is all about, habitual behavior that you don't even think about, it just happens.

Ask questions that tell you more about who they are, what's going on in their life, and what they really care about. Find out what you can do to enhance your relationship with this person. Ask them what you can do to make the relationship more intimate, more personal, and focus on what you have in common instead of what is wrong with that person or why your relationship will or will not work. Too many people focus on the problems. It is the commonalities—not the imperfections—that tie us together. When we focus on the positives, it enriches both of our lives. Nobody's perfect, but everybody has something positive that they care about. When they have the opportunity to open up and share it, to have a meaningful conversation with someone else about the things they cherish most, the stronger the relationship between those people becomes.

Keep in mind that conversations can be had through any medium, although there is a different energy when you're face-to-face with someone else. Technology is a great thing, but when you can sit with somebody and watch his or her body and facial language, it's a very different experience. I admit I am grateful for the technology we have today and use it to enhance my connections with important relationships. I have a granddaughter that lives on the West Coast and I enjoy our FaceTime conversations. The distance doesn't seem so far when we can see each other and interact in this medium. Too often, people can be in the same room or office and they will send a text or email to each other rather than have a face-to-face conversation. Conversations are what create connections for everyone. Try this exercise: Over the next 24 hours, go to a co-worker and ask your question face-to-face rather than just sending an email. Pay attention to the different connection and clarity by having a conversation. Too many people skim emails rather than read them (of course we are all busy) and this creates more misunderstanding than it creates connections.

You can apply this philosophy to anything you do in life—whether it's developing better personal relationships or enhancing relationships at work. As employers, we get busy and sometimes fail to listen to the people who are trying to get our attention—our employees. They ask questions and we give them answers, but ask yourself if you really take the time to stop, be present, and have one-on-one conversations with them. The answer is likely, "No." I make a clear choice that every day that I go to the office I make my "rounds." I talk to everyone on our team and ask how he or she is doing. I frequently ask what are they working on and if everything is going the way they think it should. I make it about them and listen to their response and ask questions if I am unclear. I believe this conveys that I care and want to know what is going on in their role with our business. I also take the time to connect with them on a personal level and talk about what is going on with their family or how their weekend was.

Too many of us don't take time to acknowledge and appreciate the hard work of our team members—we just come to expect it out of them. This complicates things and filters down into how we treat our employees. When you change direction and focus on your people—truly caring about what they're saying, what they need and what they want—your culture will transform. You will become a stronger company because everyone cares about everyone else. Your conversations become more intentional and meaningful, and the connections get stronger. Strong connections lead to greater loyalty. And when you have loyalty, you have fewer attendance problems, less turnover, and consistently higher quality work. All of these help your business grow. First, you have to care. You must get to know your team on a more personal level.

In the janitorial services industry, we have people spread out in different buildings and aren't able to see them all the time. This makes taking a pulse of the people—and clients—difficult. This is an important balance to protect. Surveys have their place, but they're impersonal and only allow you to capture a quick snapshot in time. Getting to really know your team means taking the time to engage with them, and listening to what they are saying. Whether it's a client or employee, ask them: "What do you want? What's important to you?" You can't deliver the results they want if you're not paying attention and really listening. Too much time is spent assuming we know what other people want based on our own preferences. This information is seldom correct and creates disharmony in the process.

> Learn how to disagree with others in a respectful way.

Think about it. People misunderstand what they've heard or read all the time—customers, employees, friends, and family. Once, a large client of ours wanted some very specific floor work done at night. The request was received during the day, and the notes were forwarded to the night team to complete the request.

The next morning, we received an email from our customer asking, "Why wasn't the request completed?" They were not very happy and we were frustrated.

We asked the night team and they said, "No. We did exactly what the request stated."

When we went back to the customer and asked for clarity about what was requested and what was done, we found there had been a misunderstanding—our team hadn't communicated the request correctly. The problem was that both people thought they were talking about the same thing and discovered they were talking about different areas of the building. The bottom line is that misunderstandings happen easily, but when you change the way you listen by using active listening, and then acknowledge what was just said, you're able to fix most of those issues and reduce miscommunications.

Another way to create more meaningful dialogue is to change how you ask questions. That's where a lot of the power comes from. Instead of focusing on who to blame or who is responsible, ask more questions about the situation—why did that happen and how can it be prevented from happening again? Make your team part of the dialogue, working together to find solutions. This infuses a real synergy to start getting better results on the things you want to accomplish together. When you focus on why it's important and work on the solution together, people want to be part of that kind of team.

Something else you need to learn is how to disagree with people in a respectful way. Support your team when they do something right—and acknowledge where you see success—but when you're sitting and talking with a team member about his or her performance, be honest. Have a real conversation and show you care about them and want them to be successful. They represent you and your business. If you ask them how they feel things are going with their job, listen to what they're saying and acknowledge what you've heard. If you disagree with what they said, you must be able to say so. You can't take care of your greatest asset without being honest, but you have to find a way that comes at it from the caring side versus the judging side. People respect and appreciate that.

Even when you disagree, provide encouragement—this does not mean coddle. Even if we don't agree with what they're sharing with us, there may be a component of what they're sharing that will help us look at things differently to become a better company or for me to be a better leader. I have come to realize that my employees see and hear things that I don't. When I take time to ask them and listen to their perspective, it helps me improve as a leader and provide better feedback to help them become a better employee. One of the most difficult tasks of building a team is having difficult conversations and making things more transparent. I hear all the time from company leaders that say, "Well, I don't want to say that to them because I don't want to hurt their feelings." Those who are reluctant miss opportunities to open valuable lines of communication that led to everyone's improvement. Establish a relationship so feedback goes both ways. As business owners, we can never stop learning. If we do, our businesses will suffer.

Honest conversations extend to your clients as well. Not long ago, one of JANCOA's valued customers, with whom we had been doing business for some time, was cutting their budget. They told us they could keep one-fourth of the services we provided and wanted to bid out the rest. We had ideas for this client's account that we had never expressed because we didn't think they were open to the conversation. Up until then, we followed orders rather than being a resource and focusing on the best way to achieve the result the customer wanted. We got comfortable, and they had no idea what our capabilities were.

When they informed us that they were going to bid out a majority of the work we were performing, we requested a meeting. We saw a potential crisis as an opportunity to improve our relationship. We started a meaningful dialogue with them and asked questions that had previously been avoided. We took the risk and shared our ideas and gave them options. They were impressed. As a result, they never took that business out to bid. This shows that changing direction may feel risky, but when it involves having real conversations the rewards can be very fulfilling and improve things you hadn't considered.

Another area where having meaningful conversations with others can completely change the dynamic is when we make the mistake of exerting all of our efforts toward achieving a short-term outcome just to make someone happy. By focusing on immediate results without considering the bigger picture, we end up creating more unhappiness.

We strain our relationships rather than strengthen them. We create new problems instead of solving existing ones. When we people-please, we are only creating surface value, and are putting a bandage on whatever problem we have. In the end, no one is satisfied.

Consider the recurring event in most households of a life partner who comes home from work tired, discouraged, frustrated, and upset about the day's events. They had a bad day. When the other partner arrives home, also walking in the door from work, greets their grumbling partner, and immediately suggests ordering take-out from their favorite restaurant—or they rush off to the kitchen to prepare their favorite meal, deliver a happy-hour cocktail, or suggest they watch a movie they both like. Sure, the great meal may be a bright spot in the day—but that's not going to solve any of the problems and frustration they are facing. What matters is listening, supporting and asking, "What would be helpful?" Sometimes people need to talk things through but don't want to be a burden. Opening lines of communications shows you care and it's not a burden. The best way to show respect is to listen to what someone is saying.

Rather than doing what will make someone happy in that moment, it's important to raise awareness about how to respond to situations in life and business and present solutions that result in growing deeper relationships. Early on at JANCOA, we were people pleasers. Now we take a more thoughtful approach to delivering customer service. Don't get me wrong, we want our customers to be happy, but the best way we make them happy is not by actions that become transactional. Instead, we want to benefit the relationship in the long-term rather than just making sure a client (or anyone) is happy in that specific moment, that day or week.

For example, when sustainability and "green" initiatives began to become a priority for the community, customers began asking us what we could do to cooperate with their own sustainability values. Today, our industry is faced with the challenge of changing our mindset about how we clean and what we use to get the job done. Answering the "green" call, a lot of janitorial services companies responded to customers' interest in green cleaning by simply ordering different chemicals that are marketed as eco-friendly. That is not really solving a problem or addressing clients' concerns. Does applying a different product that is labeled "green" make the service more sustainable or better? We don't think so. Sure, these products answered the client's request and helped a small part of the issue. But they're really nothing more than a surface solution. This is an example of being shortsighted rather than getting results. It's not engaging in meaningful dialogue about obstacles to be eliminated and the opportunities to capture.

At JANCOA we dug deeper and researched what it means to be sustainable—and there's a whole lot more to it than using eco-friendly products. We reached out to our people for companywide discussions about what "green" means to them and how we could implement changes to benefit our clients in the long term. We studied what successful companies outside of our industry were doing. It's important to look beyond your world and learn from others. Taking one step further shows the customer we're progressive, truly a partner for the long term.

We learned much more by listening. Ultimately, we determined that "green" is not just about the products you use, but how much product you use. The efficiency of our people on the job also weighs into the sustainability equation. We could lighten our carbon footprint on clients' properties by changing our approach to cleaning and ensuring that our employees are on board with sustainable values. Of course, all this was easier said than done. But that's the point: People pleasing is easy but it doesn't last; getting results can be difficult but always results in long-term benefits.

This may sound like complicated stuff, but it's not hard to adopt. A big part of it is great communication. People want to be heard. Talk about what they want—their needs and desires—and explain what you are doing to get results and how that will benefit them in the long-run. Articulate messages clearly, because the danger with customer service is sounding fake. Be authentic, honest, and driven by your core values. You want to be able to tell your clients: This is how I am getting information, and this is how I can help you. We want to be a resource to the customer to help them achieve their results rather than just being a service provider that takes orders.

A customer of ours told us he had executives working in the building who were concerned about bed bugs. The client asked us what we were doing at JANCOA. We explained how we were taking every measure to prevent a bed bug situation. That was a great question. We could have easily told the client we'd spray a certain product or do this or that.

> **In what ways do you show people you care? Do you pay attention to them and use active listening?**

We knew what he wanted to hear. Our relationship, however, was too valuable. We cared too much to just give him a quick answer we knew he would like. Instead, we had a longer conversation about the problem. We stopped, listened to his concern, then did research and developed protocols to address any bed bug situation we encountered. Our team immersed themselves in learning everything they could about bed bugs and cleaning practices to reduce the likelihood of an infestation. It's just like with sustainability, where we did not just pick up the phone and order green chemicals. We learned what it takes to be sustainable and responsible to exceed the customers' expectations. We learned what it takes to mitigate bed bug problems from a janitorial perspective.

Then, after we had put in the time, we sat down and presented our findings to the client, along with our action plan. We listened to each other. This built a better relationship and greater level of trust. That client knows we are truly interested in serving his best interests and we care about his people. Meanwhile, we held fast to our core values as an organization to provide exceptional service with a smile.

This isn't something isolated. Because of our commitment to engage in meaningful dialogue, we stay in contact with our customers through regular visits from our Customer Service Managers as well as our executive team. Our COO meets with the CSMs, regularly discussing obstacles and opportunities to exceed customers' expectations. Every week we hold a staff meeting where day and night management gather to connect, learn from each other, and regularly start with sharing a positive experience from the previous week. When we provide an environment to have great conversations, celebrate successes, and learn ways to improve what we are doing, that is a great meeting. Our team focuses on taking care of our customers and employees while improving the results, and that is what our culture is all about at JANCOA.

We spend time reviewing what works and what doesn't. It is imperative that we don't let the tasks involved with achieving the results prevent us from focusing on the humanity of our customers or our team. We have tried many ways of finding out what our customers' wants and needs are, including a monthly report card. It was great in the beginning, and getting scores on our performance was great to read the pulse of what was

> Your clients and employees want to be heard. Engage them, and listen to what they have to say.

happening and make the changes necessary. It became more difficult to get customers to complete the report card with the CSM present. JANCOA took the next step that so many businesses do and seem to get great results—we sent out email surveys. It gave us a chance to reach more people that were impacted by our services. I was excited about this big step in changing and improving opportunities to get real feedback.

Then reality came to us fast. We were living the statistics, and response to our surveys was 15 to 20 percent. We were told that was good. We truly wanted real information from our customers and the people that worked in the buildings we service but they were busy with their own priorities and they just didn't get around to responding to the survey. In hindsight, we can see that getting someone to complete a report card or an email survey was not creating meaningful dialogue with our customers. We restructured our CSMs territories, which gave them more time to have the conversations with the customers that had provided the success that we had experienced over the past. We went back to old school and focused on creating the environment for building a trusting relationship and having the conversations personally with the people that are important for our success, our customers and our employees. This process gave us the opportunity to also take them to lunch, strengthen the relationship and show them that we are great partners.

What's great is that we didn't dwell on what didn't work and spend a lot of time and money trying to make it work. We looked to our past and what did work and built on our history and transformed our process to get the results we were trying to achieve and improving our relationships to make them win-win. Sharing our learnings and obstacles with our team helps us to improve. Listening to the perspective of customers and team members creates meaningful dialogue that enhances relationships and results. We leave these meetings feeling encouraged and clear about ways to strengthen the relationships and improve as a business.

While getting a great report card and survey is important, it is not everything, and it's not actually the most important statistic for measuring our overall quality and performance. Our clients' decision to retain JANCOA's services—our customer retention—is the ultimate measure of our performance. That's how it should be with any business. Customer and employee retention is the most telling barometer of our success and relationship satisfaction. The longevity of our individual accounts speaks volumes in the highly competitive, price-sensitive janitorial services market. In fact, we are proud of the fact that we have customers that have stayed with us for more than 20 years. In addition to retention, that is where we grow, our customers refer other prospects to us for new business opportunities.

All of this relates to paying attention to what people are saying—active listening—through these meaningful conversations, and by providing enough communication channels so that everyone's voice is heard. It's not enough to say you care; you have to find ways to demonstrate it every chance you get. Start this new habit now. The next conversation you have, stop what you are doing, look the person that you are talking to in the eyes and practice active listening skills (listen, acknowledge, and ask questions for clarity). You will see the power of meaningful dialogue come to life—the impact is powerful.

CHAPTER 6
Think Positive

"Change your thoughts and you change the world."
—Norman Vincent Peale

One of the greatest compliments ever paid me happened quite innocently. We were in a room filled to capacity with more than 500 people when an acquaintance strolled up to say, "Hello."

She quipped, "Mary, I knew you were here because I could hear you laughing from across the room."

Laughter is a sign of having a positive outlook on life, and it's very powerful. First, it's contagious. Think about how many times you've been somewhere and heard the sound of laughter around you. More often than not that single laugh quickly spread from person to person until everyone was laughing. Shared laughter binds people together.

Laughter fills you with energy, creating healthy physical changes in your body. Laughter strengthens your immune system, boosts energy levels, diminishes pain, and reduces stress. It's no wonder that doctors not-so-jokingly say that laughter is the best medicine.

Finally, laughter creates a warm, positive feeling—both in those who laugh and those who are near enough to hear it. That's because laughter triggers the release of endorphins, the bodies naturally created "feel-good" chemicals. One of my friends always says, "Let me hear the laugh," when she sees me!

In order to genuinely laugh and create these changes it's imperative that you, yourself, are happy. Your life—and attitude—must be in a positive place so that when the laughs come, they are real. When this happens, laughter can serve as a powerful calling card.

Just like laughter, every one of us has the ability to make a positive or negative impact on someone else's life. To ensure the impact you make is positive, look in the mirror. Positive energy leads to more positive energy, and the person staring back at you is the only one who holds the power to make this happen. It's something you can't fake.

Nearly three decades ago (seems like yesterday), I made a conscious decision to have a positive impact on every person I met. I wanted my laugh to be genuine. At the time, I had just turned 30 years old, was twice divorced and the single mother of three children. Plus, I was unemployed. Then I read Norman Vincent Peale's book, *The Power of Positive Thinking*, and it really turned my head. Thinking positive was not the way I had lived my life, so I was a bit skeptical. My old way

> **Surround yourself with people who have a positive outlook rather than people with a negative mindset. Negativity can kill your culture.**

wasn't working and it was worth trying to look at the world through a different lens.

Staying positive—being able to laugh and see the potential in others— starts with positive programming. When you program yourself to think and be positive, great things can and will happen. Take care of yourself before taking care of others because everything relates back to that person looking back at you from the mirror. When his or her mental and physical health is strong, there are no limits to what's possible.

My transformation began once I stopped blaming others for my problems and took responsibility for my life. Before this, I accepted (somewhat bitterly) whatever came my way and never seriously thought about where I wanted to be and how to get there. Peale's positive thinking philosophy was a new way of looking at the world, and the more I focused on being positive, the more positive I became. I started attracting a different breed of people—those who had a more positive outlook on life, and my circle of friends changed. My stress level decreased and I was enjoying life a lot more. Something else changed, too: My sales numbers increased. Whatever it was this positive attitude was doing to me, people started noticing while I was in the field. My results were the best they'd been in a long time.

Furthermore, the more I paid attention to what was happening around me, the more I began paying attention to other people's behavior. I noticed their results and saw a direct correlation between attitude and results. It became clear that the way we think really does become the source of our energy. People who are positive have a positive buzz about them. They attract people who are happy and good things happen to them. People who are negative create negative energy and are surrounded by negativity. I wanted more positive energy in my life and so I decided to push all the negativity that had been surrounding me to the side.

This one change had a dramatic impact on my life. As a result, I started reading more books about the power of positive thinking. I learned that by changing direction with one's attitude and outlook, every obstacle would lead to a new opportunity. Life is like watching TV. We each have our own remote control. While we can't control the thoughts that pop into our head, we can change the way we choose to look at each thought—whether it's positive or negative. If the thought is negative, we can choose to pick up the remote control and change the way we approach it. The choice is ours.

Recognize that changes don't happen overnight. For most people, it's a gradual process. Making the first steps can be challenging—especially if you're surrounded by negative people. You probably do not have to look very far, though, to find someone with a great success story who exudes positive energy. Learn from them. Don't be shy to reach out and invite them to lunch or out for coffee so you can ask them about the changes in their life. Ask them how they chose to be positive and what it required to make that change. Odds are, you'll discover that you can take the same approach and achieve similarly dramatic results. It's all up to you—we live in a country where anything is possible.

Taking this first step is critical to any level of success. At the end of each day, make a list of the two or three things that went well that day. Maybe you made it to all your appointments on time. Maybe you were able to schedule an appointment with that customer or client you've been trying to meet with. Or maybe you had dinner with your children. Start looking for those things that were positive, and build upon them. Too often, people fall into the habit of pining over everything that went wrong. When you choose to identify and focus on what went right, your outlook instantly shifts. Your habits—doing the same thing over and over again—will either make things better or worse.

Next, start giving other people compliments. Something as simple as, "Peggy, you look really nice today" can go a long way. Make it a point to say "thank you" to two of three people each day. Those two small words are filled with positive energy—which can be very contagious. You would be surprised by how seldom people hear "thank you." It is a powerful way to share your positive energy.

Like laughter, positive energy leads to being healthier. It's been proven to boost your immune system and increase your overall energy. While it's not a recognized cure for what ails you, it can make you feel better. That's the true power of your mindset.

In the workplace, being positive goes hand in hand with loving your job. That doesn't mean you love every minute of every day or all the tasks that are part of achieving the results of your position. When you look at what you do for a living in a more holistic way, you either love what you do or you don't. For example, with me it's not that I love being a janitor. Rather, I love owning a janitorial service company because we're not simply focused on the task of mopping floors and cleaning toilets—though those are the tasks that are part of what we do. Instead, we focus on making a difference in people's lives, providing clarity, and helping our clients' workplaces look their best. It's about the mission we're on and the services we provide—regardless of what somebody's individual tasks are that specific day.

Think about it: Everybody interacts with other people. Everybody has an opportunity to be a positive or negative influence. Whether you are working a checkout counter at Target or you're a barista at Starbucks, you interact with a lot of other people each day. Your greeting, your smile, the inflection in your voice—every interaction you have can make somebody else's day more positive. We all have our own life and stories, and you never know what the individual in front of you or behind you is going through. Everything is connected. It's up to us to take responsibility for affecting change.

> Positive energy is contagious. When you are positive, great things can and will happen.

All of this is part of a broader movement known as Positive Psychology. It is a movement that began in the 1990s when Martin Seligman, a renowned professor of psychology at the University of Pennsylvania, published a number of studies demonstrating that when people focus on their strengths rather than improving their weaknesses they not only become happier and more successful, they make others around them happier and more successful as well. This is a real shift in mindset, and it works regardless of your profession. If I could turn the business of scrubbing toilets into the gateway to the stuff of dreams, imagine what you can make happen in your own business or life.

At JANCOA, we steer away from negativity and focus on surrounding ourselves with positive people. Tony and I take the same approach in our personal lives. It can be suffocating when you are entrenched in a work environment with negativity—people complaining about how unfair work is or resisting change at all costs. We created a magnet for the type of people we wanted to attract and the type of clients we wanted to work with. Today, we have an outstanding customer base and team of committed team members. Supporting our team members is incredibly important. So much so that a few years ago we fired a client that continually complained about our services and was on the verge of bringing too much negativity into our ecosystem.

Nothing was ever good enough for this client. Their building was one of the cleanest in our entire portfolio. We never had a problem staffing that account, and kept the staff consistent so the client always knew who would be servicing their facility each day. They worked hard, did their best, and were our top performers. We were confident in our team and we trusted their ability to deliver on our promise. This client was toxic.

They were condescending toward their own employees, and it extended to our team members working in their building. Almost

> Make a list of three areas you can improve over the next 30 days. At the end of each day, list what went well. Take time to celebrate your achievements. This action will refuel your energy to move forward.

every day, the client would find something to complain about. They would shoot off a nasty email to our manager. They berated our team members who worked in the facility and we just couldn't send the message to our team members that this behavior was acceptable. We made it clear to our team that we follow higher standards for the way we treat people—so something had to be done.

One day, I finally had enough. The negativity and stream of consistent complaints about minor issues created a toxic relationship for our team. We couldn't fairly ask our people to keep working in that unhealthy environment. Negative behavior is contagious as well; if we tolerated and accepted this behavior it wouldn't be long before we would see that spread through our business and our lives.

"We can't keep putting up with this, and our people are really suffering," I told Tony.

He agreed. Tony called the client and gave our 30-day notice canceling the contract.

They were shocked.

"You can't do that," they said. "We don't have any cleaning issues."

"Well, that's the issue," he said. "You don't have any issues but the way you treat our team is not acceptable and that is an issue."

The bottom line is that this account was a morale killer. All they did was complain—and not in a nice way. Genuine feedback about opportunities to improve are welcomed and necessary. Complaining creates a toxic environment. Tony and I agreed that we didn't want to be around people with negative attitudes—even if they were big clients. These types of attitudes are paralyzing and prevent progress.

Nobody wants to turn away business, but you reach a point where you have to decide who you want to do business with and what type of work will find you success. By standing up to this client, our team saw we supported them. Their faith in our company grew, as did their loyalty to the company, Tony, and me.

Our change in direction to be more positive also led us to see the importance of celebrating the little victories. By recognizing personal and professional achievements, you can drive each other to constantly improve. Together, we gain momentum. That's why we begin our weekly staff meeting at JANCOA with Positive Focus, where we all share triumphs that have been achieved in the past week. This makes us feel good about life, work, ourselves as individuals, and as members of the JANCOA team. We use that vital time to celebrate with each other, which also creates a tighter connection. We know each other better through the cumulative value this exercise produces.

When I reflect on the Positive Focus moments shared over the years, I am incredibly proud of our team, the culture we have created and how much we have all grown as individuals. We strive to provide an environment where our team members have an opportunity to showcase their unique abilities—and gain the knowledge, financial stability, leadership skills, and more to succeed in their careers (regardless of whether that's with us) and in their lives.

Here are some Positive Focus moments shared by our team members over the years:

My positive focus is an upcoming vacation—it will be nice to spend time with family and relax.

One day when I was cleaning, I noticed a man on the floor in severe distress. He had fallen in a place in the office where no one could see him—he was having a heart attack. I hurried over to check on him and immediately called for medical help. The gentleman was able to get the care he needed at a hospital close by. The client told me I saved this man's life. I was just happy to have been there when he needed help the most.

I'm a night manager and I supervise the cleaning of several buildings each night. One evening while I was driving down a very busy street, I saw a toddler wearing only a diaper, walking in the middle of the street. I immediately stopped—I knew I needed to get that child out of harm's way. I jumped out of the car and helped the child to safety. Then I immediately called the police and waited with the child until the squad car arrived. I'm so glad I was in the right place at the right time.

While working one night on the north side of town, I noticed a small amount of smoke from a neighboring facility. I called my area manager and the proper authorities to check it out. The fire department came just in time to avoid a major fire, which would have resulted in a significant amount of damage to our client's building.

My co-managers jumped in and helped me clean a building when I was short on help last night. I really appreciate them working with me and being great teammates.

I fulfilled one of my dreams and went on vacation to see my father in New Jersey. He has been sick, and it was important for me to see him. I have not been able to visit him for over five years.

When I was on vacation, the area managers all worked together to cover for my absence and they cooperated with and supported the teammate who filled in for me. It was a great team effort!

I noticed an office window open in the boardroom of a client's building while I was cleaning. I took the initiative to close the window and notify security. Last night, it rained very hard. That office would have been soaked with rain. We avoided a big problem.

After 10 years of working on my dream of bringing my parents to the U.S. from Mexico we finally have all the paperwork completed. During my vacation that starts this weekend, I will be going to Mexico and bringing my parents home with me. We will have our first Christmas together this year after 10 years of separation.

As you reflect upon your own life and the positive—as well as negative—energy that surrounds you, keep in mind that people love being around positive energy because it fills their own personal gas tank. The more you're able to inject positive thinking into every aspect of your life and business, the healthier, wealthier, and wiser you'll become. Sometimes, it's pretty obvious. Other times, it's more a matter of trust. The bottom line is that you just have to believe.

What areas of your life are you focusing too much energy on the negative instead of the positive?

What areas of your life are you focusing too much on the negative versus the positive of the situation? What difference would it make in your life to change the direction of your thinking and look for a positive in the situation, a silver lining so to speak? Make a list of three areas you can focus on in the next 30 days. At the end of each day make a list of something or many things that went well and you can continue making progress on with your new positive thinking.

CHAPTER 7
Don't Underestimate the Power of Desire and Faith

"Desire backed by faith knows no such word as impossible."
—Napoleon Hill

Changing direction means you crave something better than your current circumstance and have faith in yourself that you can follow through and succeed even though you can't see how it will happen—no matter what obstacles stand in your way or even if others don't believe it's possible. More importantly, you cannot let anyone talk you out of pursuing what you desire—even yourself.

When the consultant fired us, Tony and I could have very easily given up. After all, he said he couldn't help us until we helped ourselves, and that our situation was a complete mess. In his not-so-subtle dismissal, he told us we were too broken to succeed. His action shook the two of us to the core—but not because we suddenly discovered there was something wrong with JANCOA. We already knew there was a problem. That's why we hired him. Where Tony and I fell short was in the solutions department—we lacked the answers we needed to move forward. We knew our business—and our people—was hurting. We already had the desire to change direction. What was missing was faith in ourselves that we could tackle the problem without outside help. That was the spark that eventually led to the transformative solution we landed on—creating a culture focused on taking care of our team.

Desire is a strong feeling. It means wanting something you truly believe you must have. When you desire something, it's very different than simply wishing for it, waiting around for whatever it is you've wished for to simply happen. When wishes change to desire, you're finally willing to act. You step up, move forward, and actively do something that brings you closer to making your desire a reality. Desire is an aspirational goal. You can dream about a lot of things you'd like to have—some of which may never become more than a dream—but when you combine dreams with what you aspire to achieve, you begin the hard work of making your desired dreams come true. Having desire means seeing the world in a different light—as Tony and I did after the consultant fired us. Too many people just sit back and wish their life could be different instead of taking action for themselves. You need a plan.

Desire alone won't get the job done—it requires faith before the action takes place. Together, desire and faith become a powerful combination. Nobody will change direction for you—it's something you have to do yourself. Without faith, desire becomes unfulfilled. When you have a clear vision of what's possible—what you desire most—and the belief that you'll achieve it, there isn't much that you cannot accomplish. You must learn how to ignore the naysayers (including the critical voice in your head) that will tell you over and over again that you can't succeed.

I believe everyone is born with dreams. It's what you do with those dreams that separate those who are happy in their lives from those who feel hopeless. I have seen this firsthand with our employees at JANCOA—with a workforce comprised of immigrants and refugees. They've come here from other countries—many of them came to Cincinnati to escape their problems and improve their quality of life. These are people who had hopes and dreams, but more importantly they had the desire to get here. Now they are in a new country and don't know what to do next to continue the excitement about what's possible.

Many of our team members come to Cincinnati from Nepal. JANCOA is oftentimes their very first employer in the U.S. They are well educated, but have to start over again in a new country and learn the language better in order to use their education and past experience. Working with us is a steppingstone to gather where they want to be, and what they need to learn to make life better than it was in their own country. It takes more than dreams to get here—it requires a strong desire to improve life by moving to a new country and the trust that this is the right move to improve the future and make it better than the past.

This is the common thread when it comes to faith and desire—put uncertainty behind you and believe what you envision can come true.

Part of the problem is that too often we're watching other people's lives. We see what they're doing and think we want to be like them. It looks easy, we don't see the hard work and obstacles that were overcome to achieve the success they have. Unfortunately, we don't all have the same skill sets and talents. When we fail to recognize this, we begin to sink

> Desire is an aspirational goal. Combine dreams with what you aspire to achieve so you can begin the hard work of making those dreams come true.

into depression as we wonder why we can't achieve the same level of success as others. Instead, look in the mirror. Take inventory of what your skills and talents are. They are unique to you—much as they are to our team members that desire a better life in America. Relish your own personal skills and talents. Think about how much energy you're filled with and how happy you are when you use those skills and talents to do something you're very passionate about doing. Then, dream about what you can do. Find what it is you desire. Have belief in yourself that you will achieve it.

I was never on anybody's list of most likely to succeed. My path to reach where I am today definitely was nontraditional, to say the least. There were plenty of obstacles I was facing, which included not having a college degree and being a single mom with three children— it wasn't exactly the best position to start from. The first step for me was to move out of the "what my life should be" mindset to being grateful for where I was and challenging myself to pursue the dreams to create the life I wanted and would be excited to pursue. I had to change the direction of my thoughts before changing my actions. When I took the time to look beyond myself and realize how truly fortunate I was, I realized how many people I could help by working to change the direction of their thoughts and beliefs to recognize life's possibilities. My successes came when my desire to make a difference in other people's lives became stronger than just going after what I wanted in life. I came to recognize my personal skills and talents, and dreamt about how to use those to enrich the lives of those around me. I desired to make a difference. I knew that I could develop a way to make that reality. It's amazing how much energy comes with changing direction. Let's say your desire is to watch every sunrise for a month and take great pictures. You have made sure everything is ready including the camera, chair and the alarm clock is properly set. You even set a back-up alarm to make sure you get up in plenty of time. When you go to this special location you are anticipating the sunrise. There is a big obstacle—your chair is facing west, and you miss every one. It doesn't take more money or education to achieve the result that you want. All you have to do is move your chair to face east—change the direction you are facing. Determine what it is you desire and sometimes it is as simple as changing direction to realize your dreams. Believe in yourself and believe in your ability to make a difference, and you will.

Frequently I am asked why faith is so important. Faith is complete trust that whatever it is you desire is going to happen when there is no proof how it's going to happen. Faith is much more powerful than belief. It's the fuel that powers the motor that is desire. Faith is knowing that you will achieve what you want to the depth of your soul without any proof or evidence. Every day you move forward with that knowing that you will achieve your desires because you trust yourself to make it happen.

When you're unhappy in life, you may end up in a job where you settle. You settle for something less than you are capable of achieving (and less than you deserve), you become miserable. The core of what we do with the Dream Manager program is teach people to determine what they really want in all aspects of their life— their dreams—and then to recognize how to turn that into desire that becomes part of them. It's been there all along but something (friends, family, and that very loud critical voice) has told them it's not possible. As that transformation happens, they begin to believe in the possibility that they'll accomplish their dreams and live the life they've always wanted. What's more, they'll be energized to do the hard work necessary to make that happen. That's what desire feeds, that drive to move you into action. It's like putting gas in your automobile. You can't drive if you have no gas. If you want to move toward a really happy life that you will enjoy, you have to create the script for your future. You have to decide what that is and have a desire to make that happen. The strong feeling many people have of wanting something and not just wishing that you had something or were living a different life is not going to get you what you want. What is missing is moving into action and being open to learning new capabilities to improve your life. Get involved with charitable agencies or programs that would improve other peoples' lives. Expand your vision of possibilities and find someone you can share your dreams and encourage them to dream as well. When you're just waiting for something great to happen to you without any action on your part you will be sorely disappointed. When you spend a life of only focusing on yourself, waiting for others to do for you and having zero action to improve anybody's quality of life, it breeds resentment and guilt. Enlarge your circle of influence of possibility by taking care of yourself (present and future) and find a program that will feed your passion for helping others. You will change your opinion about what is possible and be grateful for what you do have in your life.

There is another side of desire that can have a negative impact on someone's life. If you watch "American Idol," "So You Think You Can Dance," or any of the other reality TV shows where people compete for success and fame, you'll see a lot of people that desire to sing or dance but don't have the talent or skill to succeed. Learn how to align your dreams and desires with your talents and capabilities you're willing to obtain to achieve them. Just because you desire it doesn't mean it's going to happen. You have to put in the work to make it happen. If it doesn't fit your skill set or talents, you either have to expand your tool kit or modify your dreams and desires to fit what you're capable of achieving. The sad thing is seeing people in jobs and lifestyles that they don't like because they're not willing to ask the hard questions of themselves. For example, "Three years from now, what has to happen for me to be really happy? What steps do I have to take to make that desire come true?"

Weigh the pros and cons of every business decision you make so you can determine what's worth pursuing and what's not.

It's crucial to have some restraint in your life, to balance reality with expectations for the future. You have today to live through. Too many people live just in tomorrow. Their desire is for tomorrow to be better, but they fail to enjoy today. Just because it's not exactly what you want doesn't mean you have to be miserable. You can have a great quality of life and still desire other things for your future. It's essential to enjoy the adventure on the route to achieving your goals—the journey can be worth it.

Not long ago I was at an event where Mark Burnett was a keynote speaker. Mark is the father of reality TV, including the hit shows "Survivor" and "The Voice." I noticed a young person sitting in the front row wearing a bright red suit. I knew that he had to have a story.

"I know there is a story behind the suit that you are wearing! Would you mind sharing?" I politely asked.

"Sure," he said. "I'm hoping to get Mark Burnett's attention. I have to be on 'Survivor.'"

"Why? Is this just something you want?"

"Not exactly," he said. "About four years ago, a good friend and I were talking about the craziest thing we each wanted to do. I told her that I wanted to be on 'Survivor,' and she encouraged me. I never did anything about it. She passed away two years ago, and now I have this strong desire to do it because I told her I would. That's why I'm here, and that's why I'm wearing this red suit in the front row." He went on to explain that he quit his job to make this his primary focus.

That made me think: Was this something he just wanted? Was it going to improve the quality of his life? Was he wasting time and energy on this one thing? I was curious if he thought beyond getting on the show and what he would have to do once he achieved the first step.

These are key questions when it comes to desire and faith: Are our desires healthy desires that will improve our quality of life, increase our energy through the experience and move us in the direction that we're destined to be in? Or are they just strong desires because of publicity, media, or something else personal that makes us feel we need to pursue it? If there's nothing really attached to the desire that's going to improve our quality of life then it's probably worth taking a step back and giving it a second look before devoting all of our time and energy toward it. I'm curious, is there a danger in creating a fantasy versus a dream? Sometimes we need to enjoy the experience and not tie any expectations to that event.

When I started working with Tony, he already had the business for 20 years, but I brought a new component to the process. By then, I had embraced being positive, so whenever something came up that appeared to be an obstacle, I would say, "Alright, this is a great opportunity." I was sure we would work it out—even when there was no proof to back it up. It starts with a mindset—if your mindset is, "I have complete trust that this is going to happen and I'm willing to do my part to help make that happen" then you've laid the foundation you need to succeed. Stay on the path you've started and be flexible with small detours along the way to reach your destination. It's like someone who joins Weight Watchers. They have incremental weight loss over time—not unbelievable weight loss that happens overnight. Too many people want the quick fix. The power of improving your quality of life and getting to where you want to be frequently occurs in incremental small changes. If you lose 20 pounds in a few months, the people you see every day might not notice, but people who haven't seen you in six months will notice it right off. Changing direction through desire and faith is very similar. You stay on track to where you want to go and keep plugging along. Before you know it, all those small changes you made along the way will add up to achieve the result.

Faith is a very powerful feeling that most people don't take the time to think about. I don't know how people live without it because it's been so big in my life. When you allow the creeping doubt in, and that critical voice starts talking to you about how this is never going to happen and who do you think you are that you could have something as special as this happen in your life, it can have a negative impact on your belief system: You'll go from being faithful to being doubtful. And that's when you're most likely to give up. You could be at step nine of 10 when that critical voice speaks up. It can get so loud that you'll stop at step nine and never take the time to focus on eliminating whatever obstacle is standing in the way of reaching step 10. This is when it's so important to trust in yourself: You're going to get what you want and you're willing to do what it takes to make it happen. While other people may want to help you do it and be rooting for you, they can't do it for you. As I've said before, every individual is responsible for his or her own outcomes in life. Even when there is absolutely no evidence that you're going to be able to take that next step, trust yourself and believe that it's going to happen anyway. Strong faith will protect you against the doubt that is always going to be present.

Many people associate faith with religion, but it doesn't always have to connect to religion. I happen to have strong faithful practice in my life and it is essential to me in the secular and religion based worlds. I know people that don't have the same belief system in their lives, but that still believe that they are going to achieve what they want in their life. Faith is complete trust that something is going to happen with no proof. It is one

Do you believe in yourself and have faith in your ability to make a difference?

of those things that is easy to connect religion with because there is no proof that a higher power exists. That there is a God and what does God really look like and what does he really want? There is no proof around God, but there are a lot of people who believe that their religion is accurate, whatever denomination they are a part of is the way that improves their life and is going to help them get the result that they want. This is a very good thing, but it's not an end-all. There are people in the religious sector that use that word "faith" all the time, but that doesn't mean it's a strictly religious word and it doesn't mean that is the way they live their life.

For me, religion is an important part of my life and a natural way of being. I start every day by praying. I end every night with a prayer. I pray several times throughout the day. Faith is knowing there is a bigger intent for my life and it doesn't matter who I please here. If I were to die tomorrow, I want to be welcomed by my creator who would say, "Well done, my good and faithful servant." So I'm doing my part to make this place we live a better place. Prayer works for me, but you don't need to be religious or pray. Take time out for reflection or meditation to connect with what it is you want and enhance your life.

It hasn't always been this way for me. Not really. For most of my life I was a people pleaser—whether it was my parents, boss, or spouses. It dawned on me one day that if I spent my time pleasing everyone I came into contact with that if I died tomorrow and my creator wasn't happy with what I did in my life, what was I actually doing? So I started focusing on doing things that made my creator happy and, in the process, started making sure I was doing the right things for the right reasons. As a result, I stopped worrying about trying to please others.

My turning point—that incredible nexus point where desire and faith meet—came when I was overworked and stressed out from trying to make every employee, customer, and family member happy with my decisions. Those were three very different silos in my life that didn't have the same definition of what I should do. I finally recognized the need to develop a different approach. My best answers to life's questions come when I have quiet time, and sometimes that's in the morning when I'm out walking my dog. I live along the Ohio River, so my best days start with a three-mile walk with my dog. It's peaceful. I fill my gas tank with encouraging energy. As I walked one day, I realized what needed to happen—it was time to take care of me instead of just doing what other people wanted me to do. I realized my own personal desire, and was inspired to make it reality.

Not everyone has those obvious moments of realization in his or her lives. Sometimes, they trust the wrong things. Misplaced or blind faith can be horrible. Watch any TV drama and you're sure to see someone who's made a really bad decision—despite believing it was a good one. Look deeper. You'll see the people surrounding them who gave them bad information, had similarly destructive lifestyles or simply had no belief in themselves. These people believed in something that wasn't going to improve their life. You see this a lot with movie stars and celebrities. Sometimes it's the clothes they wear. Other times it's a financial decision, drugs, or a relationship. We face the same situations in our own lives. Other people might be telling us what we should do, but we're not being complemented or getting the quality of life that we want because we've put our faith in them instead of our deep awareness of knowing better. We spend our time being highly frustrated and not knowing what to do next because we're waiting for somebody else to tell us what to do. That's not the way to tap into the power of desire and faith.

The best way is to stop doing what you're doing and take stock of where you are and where you want to be. Break it up into three-year increments. Look forward in your life three years from now. What has to happen to make you happy? Write this down.

Then, take more time to pause and reflect (just visit your past, do not go back and live there in your mind): What have I done in my past? How have I lived my life that is going to help me get to where I want to be? If what I'm doing is not going to help me, what changes do I need to make to get the results that I want? Write this down, too. These are frequently the most important lessons you can learn in life. What lessons do you need to keep to help you in the future and what lessons do you need to release all emotional connection from to allow you to move forward?

If you discover that you're living somebody else's dream for you, you may make them happy but you won't make yourself happy. You have to decide what's important to you and your priorities. You have to reflect on your behaviors and the choices you've made in the past—even if they are painful to admit. Ask yourself whether these behaviors are going to help you get to where you want to go? If they won't, think about what habits you need to change.

For example, if you're determined to lose 20 pounds, that's not an easy thing to do, but it is an easy goal to create because you want to feel healthier and have more energy. There are a lot of good reasons to lose 20 pounds. But here's where it gets tricky. If you look at your past and don't make changes—for example, keep eating the way you've always been eating and not exercising—you may actually gain five pounds instead. You must be honest with yourself as you look at what you desire. Ask yourself whether your behavior and the choices you make will actually help you move toward your desire. If the answer is "No," you have to recognize the changes you will need to make and trust that you're strong enough to make them.

Identify what must happen to make you happy and the changes you need to make to achieve the results you want.

In business, we talk about taking calculated risks. It's the same thing in our personal lives. You weigh the good and bad of every decision and decide what's worth pursuing and what's not. You have to get the thinking out of your head and onto a sheet of paper. Put it in some kind of document so that it's real and you can hold yourself accountable by looking at it. As long as you keep your thinking in your head and not out on paper in some format, your imagination will always distort the reality. Balance your critical voice against the one that says, "You can do anything." It all needs to be part of your plan.

Your future is going to be here faster than you think. If you don't decide what you want your life to look like, time will go by and you'll still be pining over what could have been. Have clarity in what it is you desire and the belief that you can make it happen. But you have to start today because nobody else is going to do it for you. It all comes down to the opportunities you create—and whether you're willing to believe in yourself enough to take a chance. When you are willing to take the step of blind faith and move toward your dreams you will see a big difference in the results you achieve.

CHAPTER 8
Capture Opportunities

"When I was young, all I wanted and expected from life
was to sit quietly in some corner doing my work
without the public paying attention to me.
And now see what has become of me."
—Albert Einstein

How many people can you think of who are truly an overnight success? There is really no such thing. Even Albert Einstein was a low-level patent clerk before he published the groundbreaking scientific papers that changed his life. Everyone faces tough times, but overcoming those challenges creates a path toward a better future. When you take the time to extract painful lessons from your past you create opportunities to achieve the results you want in life. Like Einstein, you are the only one who can do what you need to do.

It is your life. How often have you forgotten that? How many times have you focused on everyone else before spending a minute on yourself? If you want to capture opportunities that can change your life for the better the first step is accepting that it's your life. The second step is learning how to take the initiative. Don't wait for someone to say it's okay or tell you what to do. Sometimes, it's better to ask for forgiveness than permission. Amazing things can—and will— happen when you take the plunge.

Initiative is what changed our lives and the lives of our employees at JANCOA. We're not just in the cleaning business anymore; we're about changing lives. We want to help educate our employees and customers, and be a resource for them to learn different ways of doing things. There's no book that told us how we should do that—and I looked at a lot of books. We knew we needed to do something. We saw an opportunity, which almost always started as an ugly obstacle that needed to be eliminated. We took initiative. We tried things. Some worked better than others, but we kept moving forward. If you don't take the initiative to seize an opportunity to change direction, you will get stuck being miserable and unhappy. You'll continue to look for reasons why your problems are somebody else's fault. Maybe you'll pray hard, but you'll keep waiting for your life to change all by itself. That's basic human nature, and it will stand in your way of changing direction. Faith by itself won't get things done. Only you have the power to change your life and capture opportunities.

When I turned 30 and went through more strife than I had ever experienced, I made a huge career change. Actually, it came out of necessity (the mother of all invention) because I was out of a job at the time. I found an advertisement for a job in customer service, and it was near where I lived. It was low-hanging fruit since I had previously managed customer service reps for five years, but I needed a job. I was going through my second divorce and had three children depending on me for everything.

I went through three different interviews as part of the process, and the third interview changed my life's trajectory. It was with the company's owner and vice president, and they asked me if I would consider a different position, a sales position. They saw something in me that I had not seen in myself—possibility.

Needless to say, I was excited, but very afraid about this opportunity. It was 100 percent commission. I knew that supporting my family would rely on my performance, but settling for a job that I had done for years—even with the stable paycheck—would limit what I could provide for my family. If I went the "safe route" I would probably have needed a second job in order to make ends meet. So I took the risk and accepted the sales job.

> How often do you find yourself focused on others before you spend time seeking your own opportunities for growth?

Today, I know that if I hadn't taken that risk to pursue the more exciting—yet scary—opportunity, my life would not be what it is today. That is what happens when we capture opportunities that stretch our confidence and capabilities. What I've found is that when we are completely committed to making something work and develop the capabilities we need, our confidence gets stronger each day through our achievements.

I also know that if I hadn't taken the initiative all those years ago, I may still be the victim of so many bad experiences and would not have left that little two-bedroom apartment as a single mother with three children. I would never have met Tony. We all have the internal strength to change direction—even if something real is holding us back. One of the toughest lessons I learned in my life was that I didn't trust other people because I didn't trust myself. Everything starts with the person staring back at you in the mirror each morning. You really are the center of your universe. If you don't trust yourself, you'll never trust anybody else.

During our continuous climb from obscurity to prosperity, I had to keep telling myself that there was more to life than just money. Tony and I still remind each other of this today. We know tomorrow holds even more for us and our business if we honor our core values and lift people up as we climb toward success. Too many people attain material success without having it fulfill their lives. We didn't want to fall into that trap. Instead, we wanted to create a situation where the opportunities we had were available to others. We wanted to build a team of people who were happy, motivated, and recognized that they could overcome whatever obstacles existed in their lives in order to achieve a better future.

What I learned through this realization is that when you are happy you attract other happy people. That's a valuable lesson every employer should keep in mind. When your workforce is happy and engaged, it positively impacts your company's bottom line through efficiency and improves profitability. People want to do business with you and they want to come work for you. It's because of this philosophy and commitment to helping create opportunities for others that our fortunes changed and we continue to grow.

One of our first major employee dream success stories involved a woman named Rita (not her real name), who was in her mid-50s. Rita always wanted to own her own home—no one in her family had ever owned a house of their own. Rita shared this dream with many of our employees who rented. She wondered what it would be like to have a place to really call home.

Rita met with our Dream Manager, Joe, and told him about her goal. A big part of the program is connecting people with programs that can help—resources, nonprofits, community groups. We also help employees map out their dreams and come up with a strategy to reach their goals. We basically say: We believe in you, and want to help you.

So Rita and Joe put together a plan and he connected her with an agency that helped her establish a savings plan and took a close look at her financials. Rita felt hopeful—this could become a reality with hard work. She felt that she wasn't alone in reaching her goal. Rita stayed on course with the plan, and eventually, she and our Dream Manager were looking for houses she could afford. The agency identified a first time home ownership program that found a loan that had a minimal down payment and a mortgage payment slightly higher than her current rent. Amazed, in less time than she imagined from her first meeting with Joe, Rita was closing and moving into her new home.

When people focus on capturing opportunities and pursuing their dreams energy is created in the world that makes others want to be part of that experience. There was a tenant in the office building that Rita was supervising who found out about her new home. They always treated Rita with respect and appreciated her hard work. The tenant approached Rita one evening and congratulated her on the purchase of her new home. They asked her if she needed furniture, and let her know they were getting some new furniture. They explained that their existing furniture was still in good shape and invited her to come look at it.

That weekend, Rita knocked on their door, unsure if she should be excited because she didn't want to be disappointed if the furniture wouldn't work in her new home. As our customer welcomed Rita into their home, Rita complimented them on the new furniture. They laughed a little and told her, "No Rita, this is your furniture. Ours has not arrived yet."

Rita received more furniture than she could use in her home, and gratefully shared some with family and friends. The excitement of sharing dreams with others encourages everyone to pursue dreams and capture the opportunities. When you walk through the wall of fear great things happen creating a ripple effect that impacts others as well.

Colleagues at JANCOA watched Rita's dream come true. Quickly, the program grew more popular. More dreams became real as we continued to try and see which ways would best help our team members capture opportunities in their lives. The greatest amount of energy was created when our managers also embraced the ability to be part of a group, led by a compassionate Dream Manager, and map out their own future. The program is helping everyone at JANCOA realize that their job is a steppingstone to a better life and not a dead end. There are a lot of opportunities that they had not previously realized. Sharing one idea can help change the thoughts of possibility with others. When someone has something specific that they want to pursue, they set up a time to meet individually with Joe to create the next steps of their journey. Through achievements from members of our team, the energy and esteem grows, becoming more contagious.

If you genuinely want to help people capture opportunities, you have a responsibility to supply them with the resources necessary to realize their full potential. Provide them with resources that have the support and tools—you also need to help them look inside themselves to find what it is they are passionate about. Encourage people to take the initiative to overcome obstacles and capture opportunities.

At JANCOA, we've learned to put our employees' best interests first. It's why we have fired a couple of customers who treated them poorly or didn't share our same values. Everything is designed around being able to create as many opportunities for everyone's growth as possible—without sacrificing our morals, beliefs, or values. As a growing business we always strive to attract new clients that appreciate the

> Build a team of people who are happy and motivated by teaching them how to identify and seize opportunities, and then reward them for their successes.

benefit of having great team members work in their facility. That's the power of seizing opportunities. When you stop and make tough decisions because it is the right thing to do to protect your culture, your employees see you standing up for them and working hard to improve their lives. Their perspective of you and your business will change. Your team will look at your organization differently. They will realize how much you value the work they do, their contribution to the company, and that you do not please people at their expense. Staying true to our mission and values, we recognize that our people are key ingredients in JANCOA's secret sauce. It's a recipe we're proud to share with other business owners and individuals looking to change and grow. An essential footnote to all of this: People know if you are genuine in your actions or if it is a forced behavior. Authenticity is crucial for life to work they way you want.

It's funny. When I first started telling our story, company leaders from different industries said, "Well, my employees make a lot of money and they're highly educated so they're a little bit more skeptical than most people." I have discovered that it doesn't matter how much money you make or how high your education level. What matters are the opportunities you provide for people, and whether you help them learn how to capture those opportunities to create a better life themselves. This is where the importance of trust comes in. It is human nature to be skeptical and ask, "Can somebody really care about me that much to want to help me go after my dreams?" When you trust yourself and earn others' trust, the opportunities that open up become nearly endless. Frequently, what we see as "different than anyone else" is more about what we all have in common—humanity. We all want to be better and have more than what we have today, but the fear will cause skepticism and anxiety. I have found that encouragement gives people permission and strength to capture opportunities to pursue the life they want.

Witnessing the success of our program and the opportunities that were possible to build on that success, we realized our desire was to keep pushing change. Industry transformers never settle. They never drive in "neutral." Instead, they press forward and seek new opportunities— ways to set themselves apart from the competition. The same drive goes for individuals—when you embrace change you begin to see opportunities everywhere you look. You get excited thinking about ways to improve. Sometimes, those opportunities come from the most unlikely places.

For example, Tony and I have been clients of Strategic Coach for 25 years, and I'm honored to be one of their associate coaches for nearly 14 of those years. Being a coach has helped me change the way I look at how I do business as I help other entrepreneurs pause, reflect, and plan for their future. This opportunity came without any plan, but rather through a great conversation with my friend, Shannon, who is an essential part of the Strategic Coach team.

We were engaged in a sharing exercise that had us talking about what we wanted to do more of in our businesses and what we wanted to do less of in our time spent at work. Shannon was talking about spending less time coaching and more time creating. I was astonished!

"What do you mean less time coaching?" I said. "That would be at the top of my list for increasing time."

Shannon looked at me, a new idea forming in her eyes.

"Would you be interested in becoming a coach, Mary?"

I nearly fell out of my chair. "Are you serious?" I said. "Absolutely! What do I have to do to get started?"

Now, 14 years later, I still consider that one of the best conversations I've ever had. I still attend workshops as a client so that I'm in learning and receiving mode every quarter and can pause, reflect, and plan. I get to coach some of the most outstanding entrepreneurs from around the world that I've ever met. It is absolutely one of my favorite activities, and I feel that I always leave learning more from each session and each client. It's a win-win situation, which are always my favorite!

This may sound mundane, but it's not. Opportunities are all around you—inside and outside your organization. You just need to open your eyes and ears. At JANCOA, our people's performance is our product— and they are always surrounded by opportunities. People are the most imperative factor in our business, and depending on how we manage them can be an asset or a liability. We have worked hard at JANCOA to make our people what differentiates us from the competition. And we recognize that we need our people to put any plan into action. We just can't do it without them. That's why human resources is a driving engine behind enacting our programs, across the board. We can create a fantastic incentive program or initiate an unbeatable compensation plan, but without a strong HR team to usher these plans, and essentially guide our people, we are just tossing ideas into thin air. The people make these programs stick, and HR (remember that also means human relations!) helps these people engage in the programs. These are real opportunities for growth that we've developed—and it's all because we encourage them to take the initiative to grow personally and professionally.

Our business is also about family. We chose to build on the opportunity that presented itself and brought more family into the business. We also have many clusters of families that work with us as part of our team. Too many people see this as an obstacle because of the unique family dynamic that exists, including tension, stress, and jealousy. The reality is that there's nothing better than working with people you know, love and trust. We are building something for our family—a future for our children. That gives our daily activities a great deal of purpose, but we're humans! We're mothers, sisters, brothers, fathers, and children. Plus, our five children are from previous relationships so we have the "step" factor included. We don't always agree. We're not supposed to agree. It's funny, long before Tony ever owned a business, his grandfather told him, "Whatever you do, never hire family to work for you." Of course, there are some blessings: You can depend on your family, but they will challenge you.

We knew we needed to seek outside counsel on cultivating a strong, successful organization that will outlive Tony and me. We turned to

The Goering Center for Family & Private Business at the University of Cincinnati Carl H. Lindner College of Business. Through the center, we have attended workshops and connected with valuable resources and professionals who have guided us along this path we're walking today as we create an organization of value for future generations. Because of this, Tony and I began opening up the discussion of "What's next?" at JANCOA.

Of course, I plunged into the Goering Center full bore—that's just the way I operate when I believe I can learn more and contribute to something that will propel JANCOA forward and benefit other businesses like ours. I immediately got involved with the board of advisers and membership committee. Now, I have the honor of serving on its board of directors for a second term. I have found that when we have the intentionality and determination to make a difference, to learn and share our talents, huge strides are made in life.

Tony and I continue making valuable connections and helping others as we, too, gain insight and mature our

> When people focus on capturing opportunities, it creates an energy that makes others want to join in and be part of the experience.

business. I love this type of collaborative, passionate, creative thinking. Being involved in an environment like this has drastically changed our outlook, providing new opportunities for growth.

Why was it important to go outside of our business and tap into a resource like the Goering Center? Let's face it: When you are a tight-knit family business, you need outside perspective—you need someone to be honest with what they see, an educated audience that's watching and providing constructive criticism. This insight helped us recognize that our next generation was going to carry on JANCOA and also reinvent it. This was a very exciting and difficult prospect. It was also a great opportunity to improve as an organization and take the lessons we learned and transfer them to the next generation.

We have stressed to our younger generation in the business—assured them time and time again—that they don't have to keep running JANCOA the same way we always have. Tony and I don't want that! They can be the architects of the next JANCOA. They can filter their creativity into the business and use their talents to morph this company into one that has their stamp on it. We use the phrase "unique ability" often here because we want everyone in our organization, family or not, to recognize their special talents and put them to practice here. We want every person who works for JANCOA to be empowered to use his or her unique ability in his or her life and dreams for the future.

That can lead to some uncomfortable discussions, actually. Flashback to our first family meeting—and boy, was that a dynamic discussion. We had never held a family meeting before we began working through the Goering Center. We'd get together at holidays and actually try not to talk about the business! Sometimes that worked, most of the time it didn't. Two years ago we began holding family council meetings that include the five members of the family who currently work in the business. A facilitator leads our meeting these days, and this is incredibly helpful to keep us on task and working toward our goals.

So, that first family meeting we brought out a talking stick that I had made in a leadership class so we could take turns talking and listening. Everyone wanted to talk (of course)! Everyone has an opinion and everyone wanted to be heard because we never had a forum before. Our first meeting was a full day of addressing what each of us wanted for JANCOA and what we hoped the business would become—and how we saw each of our roles evolving as the business grew, evolved, and transitioned from one generation to the next.

The meeting was empowering and overwhelming—and some surprising conclusions surfaced. For one, the family member next in line to manage operations wasn't interested in that specific role. In fact, he was better suited to manage another area of our business. So, what seemed a natural succession of managers was rocked by the reality that our own family members were maybe not in the right place, or the place they wanted to be so they could utilize their unique abilities. Through family meetings, we reorganized some of this managerial positioning, putting the right people in the right places.

Adding complexity to this dynamic is the fact that JANCOA is blessed with a longstanding staff of dedicated managers, supervisors, and individuals working up the ranks who are not family. We work hard to give them the same opportunities and feeling of ownership in our organization.

Opportunity comes from growth—personal and professional. As a business owner that means adding employees, increasing revenue, and improving the bottom line. Our business has grown exponentially over the years. When we were less than 100 employees we managed our people much differently. Now that we have more than 500 employees, we must be very conscious of how our family and management structure cooperate. We have managers who have been with our company for more than 30 years. They deserve to have succession opportunities, too. Still, we are a family-owned business with plans to pass JANCOA to the next in line. There needs to be a healthy balance.

I remember my father telling me a story of when he had worked in another family's business years back. He recalled when the owner fired him to bring on his son who had just graduated from college. That son took over my dad's job. Sure, dad had more experience, but the decision wasn't made based on talent, skills, or unique ability. He saw this coming, but in the end, he still was more than a little surprised that he ended up on the outs after years of dedication to the business. We never want to do this to our employees—ever. Their loyalty to us is priceless, and we show our staff that by the programs and benefits we provide them that go above and beyond what is required of us as an employer. We also want our family to understand that without our valuable team, we would have nothing to pass on to future generations. So, you have to be careful about sticking to bloodlines when assigning positions in a company. Jim Collins said it best—success all goes back to having the right people on the bus and in the right seat on the bus.

Through all of this, we decided to enlist a "prosperity coach," who has a family business herself. She's an incredible adviser, and she is helping us take a look at the financial aspect of our "what's next" planning. I knew I wanted to hire her to work with JANCOA when we were on a panel together at the Goering Center and she shared how she has always loved helping grow other people's money. That's a powerful statement. She has an incredible work ethic, too, and that's a quality we relate to. Her role is to help us focus on our goals to ensure that JANCOA is a vehicle for realizing our life dreams. Tony and I eventually want to redirect our focus through continued learning, coaching others, and travel. Those are opportunities we'd like to capture. We'd like to pass the business on to our family. Just like every great athlete and entertainer has a coach to keep them on track, which is what our prosperity coach is doing for our family and JANCOA. Every business, and individual, can benefit from that valuable outside perspective from someone who can help guide you toward success. Maybe that person is a mentor, teacher, pastor, best friend, mother, or father. Maybe it's a professional

> If you want to effectively capture opportunities in your life, approach decision-making with as much clarity as possible.

coach. When we have an opportunity to share our ideas, dreams, and goals for the future, we are more likely to follow through with them—to create a plan and act on it. These are opportunities neither Tony nor I would have dreamed possible to capture because for too long we were strictly focused on survival. Once that obstacle was eliminated, it opened up endless opportunities to do so much more.

For many people, it's the same way. When we let emotions control us rather than managing our emotions for the best possible results, that impacts our life and the lives of everyone around us. We fail to see the opportunities that exist because we're focused on the problems and living in the misery. When you focus on the results you want to achieve—whether that is creating a family business that will sustain future generations, or to be the market leader in your region—then you can reach your goals. Emotions change. Opinions change. Making decisions based on others' emotions or opinions only gets short-term answers and not the results you want.

To effectively capture opportunities, approach decision-making with as much clarity as possible. That happens when we dig deep inside and listen to that voice within us instead of the loud, obnoxious voice that gets our attention daily. Learn how to be true to yourself and your goals by setting aside emotion and refraining from blaming others for your problems. Only then will you begin to build something greater than you ever imagined. This is happening now at JANCOA with our growing family business. When you're busy putting out fires, you won't have time or the ability to look at the big picture and see the opportunities waiting to be captured.

CHAPTER 9
Be Ethical In Everything You Do

"Trust your hunches. They're usually based on facts
filed away just below the conscious level."
—Dr. Joyce Brothers

Ken Blanchard has been one of my heroes for decades. When I was first promoted to a manager in the early 1980s, his book, *The One-Minute Manager* had been recently published. That book helped me learn how to manage people who had been my friends, which was not an easy transition. His lessons showed me how to change my conversation from being a peer to being a manager. It also taught me the importance of ethics.

At the time, my then-husband was very intimidated by my promotion because I was growing in my career and he wasn't. He told me in a not-so-subtle way, "I will not be managed in my home." That showed me how ethics applied to situations outside the workplace and were a way of seeing how people deal with reality through their actions as well as their words. Ethics, more than being legal, is about doing the right things for the right reasons. This can prove challenging when egos and greed get in the way.

Over the past decade, you can point to example after example of people and businesses that have made unethical decisions. From Bernie Madoff's Ponzi schemes to Tiger Woods' infidelity, these illustrate how people can abandon their ethics to make self-serving decisions lacking any semblance of principle or morality. When choosing unethical behavior, you make decisions that may benefit you financially or help you achieve what you want in life, what you think will make you happy in the short term, or might provide pleasure at that moment in time. These poor decisions fail to consider the future consequences of actions. You never stop and ask yourself an extremely important question: What legacy will I leave behind?

When you practice ethical behavior and do things for the right reasons and the right way, it serves to protect your future. You ensure a better future for yourself, your family, business, and community. Unethical decisions eventually lead to terrible consequences. They put at jeopardy anything and everything near and dear to you—whether it's in your personal life or business. This

Find ways to show respect for your team members and treat them with dignity.

is where some people get confused with ethics and make it more complicated than it needs to be. It's doing the right thing for the right reasons, a system of moral principles and values that guide your process for making decisions. Ethics demonstrate who you are when nobody is looking.

So how can you take action to be more ethical?

First, you have to be aware of who you are, what you say, and how you act. You must walk the walk and be honest in the way you live your life, whether it's comfortable or uncomfortable. For example, if you tell your children to be careful of how they spend their money, you have to do the same. You can't go out and buy yourself expensive outfits or gifts. If you tell your children not to lie, you can't lie. In order to be ethical, live by the same principles and values that you want your children to live by.

Bad things can happen when ethics break down—whether it's in your personal life or in business. Trust is a key component to ethical behavior. You can spend a long time building up trust yet it only takes one unethical action to destroy what took years to build. Take for example, corporate theft. Companies trust individuals because of their past behavior—they've shown that they are trustworthy. Being trustworthy is a character trait that companies depend on. When you're trustworthy, you begin to get more authority in the workplace. Sometimes, this means getting a company credit card. Embezzlement or corporate theft often starts off innocently enough—you put personal expenses on your corporate credit card and intend to reimburse the company. When the bill arrives, nobody in the company notices that it's a personal expense instead of a company expense. The ethical thing to do is point it out and reimburse the company. The unethical thing is to say, "Well, nobody noticed. I'll just let it slip by this one time." Eventually, it adds up and somebody notices. By that point, the unethical behavior makes it an intentional act rather than an accident and the trust you've worked so hard to build is gone in an instant.

The same thing can happen at home. How often does a spouse spend money on things that they shouldn't? The family is living on a budget and supposed to be focused on groceries and household expenses. Instead, one of them is going out shopping for clothes, outfits, or other expensive non-budgeted items. The household budget isn't working. One spouse lies to the other about how money is being spent. It doesn't take long for things to get out of control quickly.

To be ethical, you often need to look within yourself and find ways to do things outside of your comfort zone to remain true to your character. Many times, we have the strength within us that we are afraid to acknowledge. It often requires a little personal pep talk to find that strength to do the right thing because sometimes it can be hard. Several years ago we had an important customer's contact person ask us to invoice him for some work that we had not completed (or even asked to complete). Once we received the payment for the invoice we were requested to give him the money. Yes, I'm serious, this really happened. We thought we knew him well and were quite surprised at this request—so surprised by its unethical nature that Tony and I knew we had to say, "No." We also knew we had to do it in a way that would not destroy the relationship or our contract.

Tony did a great job approaching this situation. He simply told the customer that he was going to forget that the conversation had ever happened. If he requested something like this again we would have to report him. It never happened again.

It could be hard to say no to a request like this if you aren't confident in whom you are and the intention of being ethical. Be aware of these slippery slope-type of situations—when it seems you are helping someone out, but it is the wrong thing to do.

Try this exercise to remind yourself how strong you are: Remember those superhero poses where you stand with both hands on your hips, your feet about two feet apart, and stand as straight as you can? Make that pose. Now, take a deep breath in and let the deep breath out.

Stand like a superhero for two minutes. Breathe in and out. This will increase your body's blood flow. It will also give you the strength to say to yourself, "I can take this on."

We can all do what we intend to do when we decide we're going to do it. When you have a short-but-positive conversation with yourself and minimize the critical voice in your head that expresses doubt and tells you to take the easy way rather than the hard way, you will find the internal fortitude to remain ethical. It is intentional—which is the only way you can change direction in your life. Being intentional will help you achieve the result that you want and being ethical will ensure you remain the best possible person with the strongest possible character that you can be. Everyone faces temptation. Everyone has that little voice telling them that the wrong decision is the one we should choose—because it's the easy decision. We have had many instances where our team members have found money, wallets, and cellphones when cleaning a building. Customers are always surprised when we return valuable items that have been found. They always thought that the "janitor" would keep whatever they found. When you're clear on what type of character you want to display and the example you want to set for others, it becomes that much easier to reject the little voice and follow through on doing what's right. Like it or not, people around you watch what you do and how you live your life—even if you don't notice they're watching. What you do will set a positive or negative example for them to follow.

Olympian and former World War II prisoner of war Louis Zamperini once said, "All I want to tell young people is that you're not going to be anything in life unless you learn to commit to a goal. You have to reach deep within yourself to see if you are willing to make the sacrifices." That's what being ethical is all about—being willing to make the sacrifices necessary to always do the right thing.

> Being ethical means doing the right thing for the right reasons. It defines your personal character and your individual system of moral principles and values.

In business, this can be something as straightforward as whether you deliver upon the promises you make to your customers. While the customer may not always be right, they certainly always deserve respect—which means delivering the services you promise. My business life has often felt like I'm walking the line, with employees on one side and customers on the other. It's easy to get caught up in trying to make both sides happy, but I have learned the *easy* way is never that *easy* and sometimes leads to bad decisions that can haunt you. Instead, when I'm simply myself and do my job instead of acting the way I think others want me to act, I give myself the freedom to use my skills and abilities. I become more focused on creating value and making a difference based on what I am capable of accomplishing. As a result, my perspective became much more ethical—I treat people the way I want them to treat me. That may sound complicated or esoteric, but it's really just following the morals and principles that make me who I am and represent what I want others to follow.

At JANCOA, we used to do everything customers wanted us to do all the time. Today, we know that it's more important to serve as a partner and resource to raise their awareness of options to improve their experience with us. Many times, we were not asserting ourselves in client relationships—we were busy being the "yes" company. Being easy to work with and positive are "yes" qualities we want to hang on to. Saying "Yes" to everything a customer wants, even if we know it will result in poor results, is not doing anyone a service. Worse, it's not staying true to our principles.

Now, when we know a better way to accomplish a job, we make that suggestion in a constructive way, making sure to communicate to the client that our goal is to deliver the greatest value to them. Sometimes that means not saying yes—but saying, "Yes, here's another option."

Giving ourselves the freedom to share our ideas with clients has made us a more innovative and ethical company. Our clients trust and appreciate us. They don't always agree with us at first, but they want to listen to us. When we show that our ideas provide value to them, they thank us.

Being ethical extends to the way you treat others—including employees and co-workers. Look for ways to show respect and treat your team members with dignity. When you do, the rewards that come back to you are incredible.

Positive thinking and actions start at the top and trickle down. When companies tell team members what is being measured but recognize and acknowledge something very different, there is conflict. It is important not to send mixed messages. If your top priority is safety for your team then put the training and accountability in place so they can see you walking the walk. That's being ethical. Weekly meetings are critical to communicating with our team members in the field, and tracking ensures that every member of the team, from managers on down, is held accountable.

Integrity is another key part of being ethical. We realized that if we were able to be more than a service company and truly inspire change—whether encouraging employees to learn English, or delivering customer care to our clients so they feel proud of their clean facilities—we needed a strong core. Our character had to exhibit diligence, honor, and responsibility. Those are the cultural attributes we place in high esteem. That is what we strive to be as an organization. So we have tapped into the resources of a nonprofit agency called the VIA Institute on Character that educates people all over the world about their character strengths. I recently had 38 team members complete the profile and discovered 17 of 38 have "honesty" as the No. 1 character strength while "fair" and "kind" were close behind. That says a lot about our company culture. It is easier to get the results you want in your life (business and personal) when you are living out your character strengths. These are deep roots of being ethical in your life.

It's remarkable what can happen when you are ethical in everything you do. For example, today, instead of struggling to keep up in the hiring game, people find us. Nearly 60 percent of the people we hire come to us through referrals of current employees. While we recognize that the Dream Manager reputation is part of it, we can't overlook the fact that we have become known as a very ethical organization. It's how we know we're doing something right. We've had as much as 17 percent of our referrals come from previous employees. They appreciate the way we treated them when they worked at JANCOA and show their appreciation by sending qualified candidates our way. Referrals are the best hires we make. We can be almost certain that a referral-hire will fit into our company culture, and they already know what JANCOA is all about. We don't glamorize our industry. The job is what it is: You are cleaning buildings. You work hard, scrubbing, sweeping, dusting, and meeting high expectations in every task. However, the extras we provide our employees make the experience one that has a great impact on their lives. We know that the image and quality of our employees determines our success, so we invest in our people by helping them improve their quality of life with a meaningful job and the Dream Manager program while serving as a resource and partner to our employees.

One of our core principles is the value of teamwork. We work in teams. This team structure is key for accountability and morale. Each building is considered a team, and our office support and night management staffs are separate teams. Teams support each other to reach our common goals of quality, budget, and retention. Depending on the size of the account, a building team may be broken down into smaller teams. The teams work in concert because of constant communication and visits from our management team to keep everyone on task and apprised of the clients' goals and any feedback we have received. Our teams know they are responsible for meeting the goals of their respective buildings and that their actions represent our company as well as themselves. We trust them and they trust us.

Look within yourself to identify ways to step outside your comfort zone and remain true to your character.

Refreshing our company culture and focusing on being a company that serves others has changed our destiny. That's not to say that we weren't ethical before, when we faced all those challenges. It's just that we became much more cognizant of what we were doing and, as a result, more intentional in our ways.

Keeping a positive attitude and walking your walk every day is influential in any organization. It leads to a gratitude attitude, where as an employer you recognize that your role is to provide employment, fulfill a service need and, most important, serve people. You also need to be grateful and have fun while you're doing this. Being ethical doesn't mean being boring. In our case, we want our people to believe in the work they do for JANCOA, and so we have adopted the FISH philosophy practices from the book about boosting morale and improving results:

- Be there: Be present at every moment.
- Play: Have FUN while being responsible for the result.
- Make their day: Make a difference in someone else's day.
- Choose your attitude: A positive attitude can make a bad day a better one.

We expect our employees to give their best on the job—which is a reasonable expectation for any employer. When our employees are on the clock, they are giving back to our organization. They do this wholeheartedly because they know we care enough to help them in their personal and professional lives. Again, because we're ethical, they trust us and know that we're all working together. We all want to be better every single day. It becomes a sign of respect when they show us that they're here to work and do their very best. They know we appreciate them because of their dedication. Being "present" on the job improves communication and ultimately strengthens relationships with our clients.

One of our core principles is being creative. We encourage our people to be creative and enthusiastic—to play with ideas and find solutions. We make a point of letting every one of our employees know that their ideas are welcome and that we take their input seriously. Then we say thank you to them with simple gestures and recognition. Everyone needs to spend a little more time pressing the pause button and celebrating successes—and we're no different. Let's face it, when you make someone else feel good, you feel good, too.

Ultimately, your success in life is dependent on your ability to take responsibility for your actions. When you wake up in the morning, you decide how you will take on the day's challenges. You are responsible for making your own day. If it is to be, it's up to you—that's the essence of the gratitude attitude.

Look around you and work to instill that attitude of self-reliance in everyone you interact with. When people are empowered to seize the day, they bring that energy and focus to everything they do. When combined with encouraging others to always do the right thing, everyone benefits.

Keep in mind, however, that people are not perfect. You will make mistakes, and you may find yourself toeing the line between being ethical and unethical. Even if you find yourself beginning to stray from the ethical path, it's still possible to regain your footing. It requires strong communication and being honest with yourself. Too many times, we try to put the blame on somebody else for our actions: "If so-and-so hadn't have done this, I wouldn't have done that." But when you're able to look yourself in the eye in the mirror, the only person you can blame for your behavior is you. Being responsible for your own behavior is the biggest thing you can do to remain an ethical person.

From my perspective, I'm on my third marriage. I could offer up dozens of reason why it is my first two husbands' fault that those marriages failed. But I had something to do with those failures. It takes two people to make any relationship work—whether it's a marriage or an employer-employee relationship. If you truly want to leave behind a legacy that matters, you must learn how to have those difficult conversations in life. Tough conversations can make a relationship stronger, deeper, and more enjoyable. If your goal is to be ethical, you're going to have to have uncomfortable conversations and realize you're never going to be perfect. You're going to have to learn how to say, "I made a mistake. This is how I'm going to fix that mistake. This is what I'm going to do to prevent that from happening again."

> Who are you when nobody is looking, and what legacy will you leave behind for others to remember you by?

Remember, being ethical means doing the right thing for the right reasons. Your ethics define your personal character and individual system of moral principles and values. It means being able to ask yourself the most crucial question in life: Who am I when nobody is looking?

Now, it's your turn to go to the mirror and ask yourself that question. If you don't like the answer, or what you see, it's not too late to change direction in your life. That is the best part; it's never too late to change direction. Ask yourself, "Who do I want to be?" and "How do I want to be remembered?" The answers may surprise you but will become a new guide to help you make choices that stay within ethical boundaries.

CHAPTER 10
Take Care Of Yourself

"Trust yourself. Create the kind of self that
you will be happy to live with all your life."
—Golda Meir

It may sound selfish, but the truth is you are the center of your own universe. You have to take care of yourself because no one else is going to do it for you. This means scheduling time to take care of your physical needs and emotional health. What you eat, when you sleep, and how often you exercise impacts your well-being. The information you feed your brain through what you see and hear impacts your mental and emotional health—including how you behave. The bottom line is that changing direction is really up to you.

People often view physical and mental health as two separate things, but they are connected: When you take care of yourself physically, your mental health improves—including your emotions. Emotions matter because they are directly related to behavior. If you're unable to manage your behavior it leads to problems. It doesn't take much to destroy everything you've worked so hard to build up in your life. Taking good care of yourself improves your thought process and decision-making capability. The decisions you make affect quality of life and your attitude about your quality of life impacts your happiness.

Another effect from taking care of yourself is that you have more to look forward to in life. I've come to believe over the years that when people don't have anything to look forward to they start looking to the past. They get stuck thinking about what could have been. That's unhealthy because it can become the root of a lot of problems. Too many people look at the past and either focus on all the bad things that have happened and use that to assume a victim mindset; or they believe with all their being that it was the best part of their life and it will never get better. For example, I know someone in their 60s whose best time of their life was when they played football in high school. When you have a conversation with him you would think his life literally stopped after high school. This is a big reason why dreams are so important: They provide something real to be excited about and a reason to look forward rather than backward. Our past is a great place to visit when we want to extract a lesson from an experience and use it to move us forward toward the bigger future we want in our lives, but the past must remain in the past.

Years ago, as a single mom, I learned this lesson the hard way. At the time, my ex-husband wasn't providing support to our family so I had to take care of our three children by myself. I was a 100 percent commissioned salesperson, which meant I worked as hard as I physically and mentally could in order to make ends meet. To say I burned the candle at both ends would be an understatement.

My oldest daughter was 13 years old. I pressed her into duty to help out with her two siblings as much as possible, but nearly everything fell on me. I followed the same routine every day: Work while my younger two children were in day care and she was at school; go home to make dinner and take care of anything else that needed to be done around the house; put my children to bed; and then go back to my office to get more work done. Maybe I would get a few hours of sleep—if I was lucky. In the morning, I would wake the children, get them off to school, and start the whole process again.

I wasn't very healthy back then—mentally or physically—but I was successful in my career because I had to be. Sales were good and my boss gave me accolades for the work I was doing. I couldn't depend on anybody else, so I was very focused on work. For a while, this situation worked. Unfortunately, you can only get away with an unhealthy lifestyle for so long. In my case, exhaustion finally became too much to handle.

By that point I had started dating Tony and began to transfer all those skills I'd learned into working with him. Once we married, we started blending our two families. We were working with a counselor to help us, and she became the catalyst for my change. The counselor noticed how unhealthy I was and finally said to Tony, "This poor woman is exhausted. Let her go home and sleep for three days."

All of a sudden, I had someone to support me—Tony—but I had never found the time to take care of myself and had to learn a whole new way of doing things. First, I had to learn how to relax. It's something I never had time to do. Then, I built teams of people in the workplace to do things I didn't do well and delegated. That meant learning how to work smarter—something I'd also never had the luxury of doing before. Once those things happened, I started addressing my personal health.

> Help people be successful by treating them like assets and looking out for their physical and mental well-being.

Most of what I've learned came the hard way—which isn't the best way to learn when it comes to your health. No matter what your individual situation is, know that you can have a great career and family life without pushing yourself up against that exhaustion wall and jeopardizing your mental and physical health. If you learn how to feed your body and mind before reaching the point of exhaustion, you'll be much happier.

It's no secret that we live in a faster-paced world than we did just a decade ago. We all have the same 24 hours each day, but it seems to go faster and faster every day. That's no excuse for failing to take care of yourself. Being busy is something everyone deals with, whether you are an executive, stay-at-home mom, high school or college student, or someone just starting out on a career. According to Dr. Ned Hallowell, founder of the Hallowell Centers and the world's foremost authority on attention deficit hyperactivity disorder (ADHD), if you don't have ADHD you are still living in an ADHD world. Everybody is moving so fast and trying to jump from activity to activity that they're distracted from what is really important in life. This distraction often keeps people from experiencing a higher quality of life because they're not able to stop and focus on what their priorities should be. Being busy too often distracts us from taking care of ourselves and we end up putting "self" last instead of first.

Years ago, I thought I could do it all. Today, I know I can't. You can have it all, just not at the same time. Instead, you have to be present wherever you are. If you are spending time with your children, you need to be completely dedicated to that experience. If you are at work, focus on your job or your career without wondering what's going on at home. Sure, we all wonder what's going on at home, but is there really anything you can do about it while you are gone? So be present wherever you are. It's remarkable how when you prioritize your life each day—sometimes adjusting priorities throughout the day—you spend time doing what you should be doing. You focus on the results you are trying to accomplish. When you try to do everything all at once, the balance tips and you crash, negatively impacting everything else in your life.

So how can you maintain a balance? How can anyone effectively juggle a family, career, or even a payroll for employees who depend on him or her for their livelihoods (the life of an entrepreneur, making sure there is always enough money in the bank!)?

The key is to stay F.I.T. and move forward with focus, initiative, and trust.

Focus means keeping your eye on the ball. That doesn't mean just being focused on a task, but being focused on what you want and what you are made to do. This is where the Dream Manager program comes into play. If you are not sure what you want in your life, business or career, you are simply accepting what comes into your life. If that doesn't make you happy, then you end up depressed. Way too many people feel depressed because they are not happy with the way life is going. You can change your path by getting focused on what you want. Every one of us is born with dreams and the talent and skills needed to achieve those dreams. The adventure of life is bringing those pieces together, because when you marry your dream with your talents and skills, that's when passion begins. We've all known people in our lives or seen people that have great energy and great passion, and we feel a little bit envious because we would like to have that same energy. One of my favorite memories is seeing Barbara Mandrell in concert. Many of you may not even know who she is, but she was a wonderful singer and entertainer. At the end of the show, I stood to applaud her, appreciating the wonderful gift she shared with the world. From what I have read, that was always her dream and she went after it no matter what tried to stop her. That's a product of being focused.

One way you can get more focused is by feeding your mind with inspiration and positivity. Engage with people who charge you up rather than drain you. Guard your time and energy carefully and prioritize your activities. Find ways to escape so you can dream and think. For me, that can mean a brisk walk—maybe I'll listen to a spiritual podcast during that time, or just listen to the cadence of my steps moving forward.

Next, each night, make a list of three things that need to happen in order for the next day to be a success. Then, at the end of that day, write down three things that went well—your big wins. As you repeat this exercise daily, you'll work toward what you want to achieve in life and business and be much more focused. Reacting to the daily fires that happen gets us off balance and takes away our focus.

These days, Tony and I are focused on our family succession plan. Not long ago, we took a long walk together and talked about where we envisioned our lives 10 years in the future. These types of conversations are important. We thought about what we'd be doing if we were not tied down to anything, including the business. What would get us excited? Have you asked yourself this question? In high school and college, we talked about what we wanted to be and what we wanted to do. We dreamt about what we would become. That thinking stopped along the career path, which is why dreaming is so powerful and important to me, personally. It doesn't matter where you are in life or how old you are, you must

Do you maintain a healthy balance among family, career, faith and other activities in your life or are you burning the candle at both ends?

have something that gets you excited about what's next. You have to focus on that dream and excitement.

Think about Diana Nyad, a world record holding, long-distance swimmer who became the first person confirmed to swim from Cuba to Florida without the protection of a shark cage—swimming from Havana to Key West. Diana was intensely focused on her goal, and she achieved it on her fifth attempt. Her team wore T-shirts that read, "Xtreme Dream." I love that. She knew she could not complete this goal by herself. When we try to do everything ourselves we frequently end up frustrated and no closer to the dream we want to achieve. There are too many things that we need to focus on to complete them all properly. Whether you are at home taking care of your family and home, a professional building a business, or a sportsman going after the undoable record. Creating a team to help is imperative to achieve what we want. Diana knew that to achieve her dream she had to have the right team and trust in herself to put that team together. It's so important to know who you are and trust yourself. You are made to do something—the hard part is listening to that inner voice (the positive one!), then focusing on the task at hand, and trusting your gut.

Focus is critical for success, but you won't get anywhere without initiative—the second part of being F.I.T. Tony and I took the initiative to create a unique employee engagement program at JANCOA that encouraged people to dream. We wanted our people to have something to get excited about in their lives, and to go after their aspirations. The key is "go after." We don't make their dreams come true—we empower them with the tools, resources, and support to get them on their way. The work is up to them. Tony and I felt the work was up to us to create a program to help our people be more engaged, successful workers, which in turn would improve our business.

Successful companies take initiative to help their people be successful. They treat their people like assets, by encouraging and engaging them to get them excited about life. There are too many companies that have a toxic culture where people do not feel valued. Ultimately, successful companies create value for the world, and for individuals. When you create value, you get rewarded. You get F.I.T.

I shared the definition earlier that initiative is the ability to think and solve problems, and then take action by thinking of the solutions rather than being told what to do. I can't think of a better example of this than Malala Yousafzai, author of *I Am Malala* and the youngest person to win a Nobel Peace Prize. Malala is a fierce advocate for women's education. She says we don't learn the importance of anything until it is stripped from our hands. That is what happened in her hometown in Pakistan when the Taliban moved in.

Women were not allowed to go to school, or to go to the market. They were confined to the four corners of their homes. Since the real terrorism began in Pakistan in 2007, she says hundreds of schools have been bombed and women flogged and slaughtered. Signs were removed from schools. Malala, then 14 years old, spoke out publicly against the Taliban. She raised her voice. She wanted to tell the world what was happening and that women in her country were suffering. She took initiative and put her life on the line, literally. She survived an assassination attempt in October 2012. She's still a target for the Taliban, but her passion for women's education and rights drives her forward. She's selfless in her pursuit. When asked what she would do if a Taliban assassin came calling again, she told a reporter: "I'll tell him how important education is, and that I even want education for your children as well."

The last step of being F.I.T. is trust. You really have to trust yourself in order to succeed and realize your dreams—or to dream at all. Dr. Joyce Brothers says, "Trust your hunches. They're usually based on facts filed away just below the conscious level." We have to discover what we are meant to do, go after it, and trust our abilities. We have to trust other people to help us along the way. Life is a team effort. Whenever we doubt others or feel uncertain about a situation, usually the reason is because we do not trust ourselves. Look inside. Look real deep. Listen carefully for that voice. Let it rise to the top, and follow the lead. You'll be much better off for it.

When it comes to issues that affect our health and well-being, the No. 1 factor that brings us down is stress. In the workplace, people who just want to do a great job cause most of the stress. Stress is an internal issue. We create our own stress and allow external things to internalize within us. It's up to us individually to determine how we're going to let that affect us. When it comes to changing direction, it determines whether we're going to face the sunrise or the sunset. Just as important, when you embrace change you put yourself in a position where you can begin to effectively think about the future and start dreaming. Only then can you begin to leave the stress behind.

Does this mean you have to turn off the rest of the world in order to be F.I.T. and take care of yourself? No. Sometimes you don't have the luxury of doing that. In the middle of a crazy day, you may only have time to go into your office, close the door and take a five-minute breathing break. Turn off the phone and take five minutes to close your eyes and take a few deep breaths, breathing in and breathing out. Visualize your happy place with the breathing exercise. It will bring oxygen to your brain and allow you to visualize whatever circumstance is taking you to that time where you need to breathe easy. What do you want the expectation to be? How do you want the situation to end?

Learn how to feed your body and mind before you reach the point of exhaustion and lose your focus.

Visualize it and what you need to do to get there? If you do have the time, go to a fitness center, take a walk, or try yoga. Breathing is the key to relaxation because it creates equilibrium and balance.

One tool I shared with my management team is creating a vision of smelling the flowers and blowing out a candle. This exercise helps you slow down. When you move too fast, your breathing changes. You don't get enough oxygen to your brain—which changes how you process things. When you don't think clearly, you don't make good choices. Everything is connected. If you can take a minute to smell the flowers and blow out the candles the oxygen flows better to your brain and you respond differently to everything going on around you. This simple exercise can make a huge difference.

Another trick is to stop and take a breath before you answer the phone instead of answering it while you're in the middle of finishing a sentence or a thought. It will give you a moment to slow down and focus, which changes how you react and respond on the phone. This can be used everyday, all day; pause, take a deep breath and move forward. The clarity will reduce frustration and stress. You will trust yourself more because you are connected to your core and not reacting to something that is happening to you or around you in any circumstance.

Slowing down is an important part of being F.I.T. A great mentor once told me, "Mary, nobody is going to tell you that you can't use the restroom if you say, 'Excuse me a minute, I need to use the restroom.'"

That was a valuable lesson, and it applies to much more than taking a bathroom break. Sometimes, you just need a few minutes to catch your breath and bring your equilibrium to where it needs to be so you feel you're best and most confident. It's your world and your choices, and you don't have to be rushed 24 hours a day,

> Get F.I.T.: FOCUS on the results; take INITIATIVE and take action; and don't forget to TRUST yourself in the process.

seven days a week. There comes a time when you realize this—when the signs become so clear that you can't help but notice something is wrong. People have been known to put their telephone in the freezer or lock their keys in the car. Making silly mistakes that make no sense can be a sign that you're not taking care of yourself. If you're going too fast in the car and don't normally speed, that's a sign. Putting words together that don't make sense or not remembering something you always remember are signs you are moving too fast. When you start making bad decisions at work or have a short fuse with colleagues, heed the warnings that you need to slow down and focus on yourself.

Another problem is over committing yourself. Think about the child who is rushed from activity to activity without a break. Executives often run into this problem because they have a tough time saying "No." We all want to give back and help others, but it can reach a point where you become so focused on doing things for others that you forget to do something for yourself. Saying "No" doesn't make you a bad person or mean you don't care; it just means you recognize you can't be everything for everybody—no matter how much you'd like to be. I've said for years, "If you make all of your decisions based on your brain, you are perceived as an uncaring person. But if you make decisions with only your heart, you might not make very good choices." There is a reason we are born with a brain and a heart—they balance each other so we can consciously make good choices.

The people who do a great job fostering their mental and physical health have learned how to strike a balance in their lives. Make no mistake about it, changing direction in your life isn't easy and requires work. And even if you're able to address all the other issues that stand in your way, you'll still never make your dreams come true if you don't learn how to take care of yourself. Start the new habit today of being F.I.T., **focus** on the result, take **initiative** and **trust** yourself in the process.

EPILOGUE
A Dream Mindset Changes Communities

"All organizations say routinely, 'People are our greatest asset.'
Yet few practice what they preach, let alone truly believe it."
—Peter Drucker

resident Woodrow Wilson once said, "We grow great by dreams. All big men are dreamers. They see things in the soft haze of a spring day or in the red fire of a long winter's evening. Some of us let these great dreams die, but others nourish and protect them; nurse them through bad days till they bring them to the sunshine and light which comes always to those who sincerely hope that their dreams come true."

Dreaming, as Wilson asserted a century ago, is really the underpinning of changing direction. So many times, dreams are never realized because we don't have the courage to step outside our comfort zones and make the changes needed. It's hard to stop mourning what could have been, take control of our lives, and start dreaming about the future. It's even harder to take action to fulfill those dreams. Let's face it, changing direction isn't easy; sometimes, you need encouragement and a helping hand. No one should be a victim of his or her circumstances. It's your choice to embrace change, eliminate obstacles from your life, and capture opportunities—no matter how bleak the situation seems. It's never too late!

Look at my life. After a couple ex-husbands and an unconventional start with a few detours and roadblocks, I had accepted a victim mentality. I never thought my life would amount to much more than being a single mother working her butt off to make ends meet. Because of a boss who believed in me and was willing to invest in my development, I chose to change my mindset. I started to believe in myself and saw the need to change direction. This led to a chance meeting with the man who would become my husband, my life partner, and best friend. Nothing has been the same since then. Life is a series of crossroads and decisions you make. The choices I made—and the people whom I met along the way of my own personal transformation—changed my life for the better. It's really no different for you.

As we've discussed, there are 10 choices you can make today that impact your dreams. By taking control of your life and choosing to take action, you can learn to dream again and change direction in your own life. Dreams are for everyone.

Once you embrace change—something that on the surface may seem difficult—you've taken that critical first step, and you're on your way. Next, eliminate the obstacles in your life so you can have a more positive and optimistic view of the world. Part of this is recognizing that people don't fight over dreams about the future. They fight about problems of the past. In some cases, too many of us think that our parents, friends, or loved ones are "dream killers" when mostly, they are afraid for us because they have not achieved their own dreams. This is an important bridge to cross because when we allow fear and disappointment to dictate our direction, we cannot move forward. We simply go through the motions every day rather than going after what we really want in life. You must break through that barrier if you're going to change direction.

So ask yourself and those around you, "What do you want in life? Where do you envision your life, career, 10 years from now?" Take the time to write down your dreams—it gives them life.

Everyone who wants to change direction in his or her life needs to take the time to dream. But it requires something more—choosing to take action. Focus your dreams into achievable goals, and develop action steps to make those dreams reality.

With JANCOA, the Dream Manager program came about because we were aiming to solve our people problem and help our employees improve their lives. It was a reflection of the personal choices I made and applying them to our business. As we built it, the program became much bigger and I recognized the impact of helping people learn how to dream and change direction. This concept is contagious. We all want to feel better about our lives, to do meaningful work—to be excited about what's next, all the possibilities.

Matthew Kelly's fictionalized book about our efforts, *The Dream Manager*, caught the attention of a lot of people. We received emails and letters from business owners all over the world who were starting to put the Dream Manager program to work with tremendous results. One company, Netsurit, an IT support company based in South Africa, got a copy of *The Dream Manager* and, in the process of implementing the program found that their culture shifted.

Today, they live by the cause, "Supporting the dreams of the doers." They support their employees as much as possible to reach their dreams. Netsurit started a dream management program for employees with dream facilitators who encourage and motivate employees to dream, and achieve their goals.

This mindset has turned out to be a competitive advantage for Netsurit, as well as many other organizations that have adopted ways to help their employees dream. In nearly every case, it's also helped them attract top talent and win clients. That's because when you marry the personal impact of changing direction and dreaming with its business applications, there is no limit to how powerful this idea can be.

In our own backyard, Talbert House, a Cincinnati-based nonprofit social services agency, launched a program with the hope of motivating its people, which would in turn give them the energy and confidence to work with clients who are in transition, including incarceration, addictions, or mental health issues. This came about after one of the directors of Talbert House participated in a Leadership Cincinnati class where I was involved. Our class had to complete a project that would help create value in the community without creating a whole new nonprofit. So, we created an entry-level program that would be cost-neutral for nonprofits.

Talbert House embraced this project and put it to work in its organization. The results have been truly inspiring. The president and CEO sent an email about how the program impacted his people and the people that the nonprofit serves. He wrote, "I wanted to let you know about something that happened to me today. I visit our 40 sites on a rotating basis and visit a site every other week. Today, I was visiting with staff at our downtown location and two case managers told me along with the entire group of 20 staff about their wonderful experience with Dream Manager."

The *Readers' Digest* version is, they loved the program. It changed their perspective about their current job, future career possibilities, and beyond. They also said it changed how they saw clients' aspirations and dreams. It made them want to encourage their clients to have more hope about their own future. Needless to say, that comment made my day, if not the entire week! It demonstrated to me that the idea of embracing change extends far beyond the walls of any organization and can transform individuals' lives collectively as opposed to one at a time.

As I spend more time sharing ways people can change direction in their lives, I always appreciate hearing these success stories. If I'm able to inspire just one person to take control of their life and begin to see a better future more clearly, I'm achieving my dream.

Perhaps one of the most powerful aspects of being able to dream is this ripple effect: When people achieve their dreams, they want to help others do the same. They want to "do good," and begin looking for ways to help. When organizations help people see the world through a different lens, they're essentially building an army of people who will carry it forward on their own time and in their own personal and professional networks.

Rita, who I talked about earlier, purchased her first home with the help of JANCOA's Dream Manager program. She was empowered with the tools and resources to make it happen. She had the courage to dream, the determination to work hard, the initiative to save and work with the resources provided to her. She trusted in others and in herself to make her dream a reality. Her outlook on life changed completely because she accomplished something she never imagined was possible. It was natural for her to want to help others reach their goals and make better lives for themselves.

Rita started a canned food drive at the building where she was supervisor and asked all of the people who worked on her cleaning crew to bring in food and clothing. The goods were going to be donated to an employee's family in Guatemala. Rita had been talking to this employee about the holidays—this worker had been sending home all of the money she earned to help support her family, but it was not going to be enough to give them the type of holiday meal or clothes that they needed. This touched Rita's heart. She wanted this family to have joy during the holiday season, so she took the initiative to collect needed items to send to them. Because of Rita's initiative and the generosity of her team, this family had a wonderful Christmas.

I was so proud of Rita—and I approached her.

"Rita, you've never done anything like this before."

"Well, I never owned a home before!" she said. "I never thought dreams like that were possible."

Rita showed how when good things happen to you, you want others to benefit, as well.

Dreaming creates a chain reaction of positive energy and cultural transformation—both on individuals and society. The idea we hatched at JANCOA in a time of utter desperation, when we were truly in a great deal of pain because of our turnover problem, became a blueprint for creating a better work environment that attracts top talent and a model for others to follow. Whether in business or in life, that's what happens when you teach people how to take control of their own lives—it changes how they look at things and, as a result, you end up changing your culture while they end up changing their outlook on life. When your culture changes, it has a direct impact on your bottom line—enhancing employee engagement and retention. It also improves the quality of life of everyone involved. When your outlook becomes different, you embrace change and can imagine a different future.

At its core, changing direction means being open to embracing change—not fearing or running from it. It becomes part of who you are and how you live your life.

Sometimes, on the way to a dream, you alter your course and find a better path. That's what happened to Tony and I. When our grandson was 5 years old, he showed us exactly what JANCOA meant to the family and their future. One morning at home, he had dressed himself in a pair of khaki shorts and a clean white shirt and announced to his father, "I'm ready to go to work, dad."

Our son was caught off guard and said, "You look great, son! But, I've got a lot of meetings today, so I can't take you."

The little guy was so upset. He had a tear in his eye and a planted smile on his face, but with a determined look reminded our son, "You said the next time I have a day off school I could go to work with you. I don't have school and I'm going to work with you."

Well, that was that. Our grandson came to the office that morning, and as our son pulled into our parking lot, our kindergarten "intern" exclaimed, "I can't believe we're really doing this!" He wanted nothing more that day than to see where his father, grandparents, and other family members went to work. He wanted to know what was going on while he was at school, what we were talking about at the dinner table, family get-togethers and so on. He wanted to see JANCOA for himself. He wanted to be part of this.

That day, I took a great picture of Anthony D. Miller one, two and three in the conference room (that's my husband Tony, our son—also Tony—and grandson, who we call Trey). When I printed out the picture, there it was in plain view: Our family business had grown from a job Tony started in college, to one where we all work in a business with a career path, providing opportunities for the future generations of our family and employees' families. I realized that every choice we make as a business impacts Trey, his siblings, his future, all of his cousins, and family not even born yet. Succession planning wasn't our initial dream for the company's future, but it quickly became the new one.

Now we are focused on grooming JANCOA for future generations by creating programs for our people, drastically improving our employee retention, focusing on servicing our customer "sweet spot," and continuing to build an infrastructure with systems that ensure quality and consistency. Before, our goal was to be able to sell JANCOA and retire. Our new dream is to create a legacy and a great source of pride for our family as well as the JANCOA family. That realization changed everything.

When you stop and think about the power of change, it can be such an enlightening moment. Many of our employees (including family) came on board because they just needed a job. Now they see how we are creating a business of value for employees and customers, while changing people's lives. More and more people want to be a part of what is going on here. All this positive energy creates a boundless momentum. Imagine your own business or family generations from now, even a couple hundred years down the road. Think about how the decisions you make today and how they could impact your future grandchildren and their children, your cousins and fourth cousins, and so on. It all goes back to the concept of beginning with the end in mind. If the end-goal is something that will last for generations, then how are you working toward taking small steps that may create a lasting impact?

Every day, I am writing a new chapter for my own life story. At the same time, we are writing our story here at JANCOA. Each week is a fresh chapter. We learn things the hard way. We take away valuable lessons from mentors and through our involvement with community groups. We hear from our people what's working and what's not. We learn that we are making a difference in our employees' lives. We ask ourselves, "How can we do more?" It's so easy for you to do the same thing—you just have to take action.

Learn how to take hold of your dreams and achieve them. Open your eyes to what's possible and you'll find that you've changed direction— you'll see you are facing the sunrise, and with it, opportunity. If you start with a few choices, try these three to begin your journey:

- Work on your own dreams.
- Share your dreams with your friends and family.
- Learn how to embrace change personally and professionally, and encourage others to do the same.

Life is an adventure. There is always a new path to explore. When you acknowledge your dreams, utilize the talents and skills that you are born with, and allow yourself the opportunity to pursue your dreams, you will begin to see and feel your passion come alive. In doing so, you can—and will—become the person you were meant to be, bringing value to the world and to people around you. Together, we will all start enjoying the process of living rather than simply wandering through life. We will want to help others achieve the same result. Now it's your turn…focus, take the initiative, trust yourself, and change direction. You'll be happy you did.

Acknowledgments

There are many people who say, "Write a book" as if it is as simple as walking down the street. My experience has been a bit more of a complicated process, taking more time than I had expected. I take special note that I have repeated that pattern a number of times in my life! I acknowledge that this would never have happened at all without the help of some very key people in my life.

Every book has a beginning and that would have to include Dustin S. Klein. He is the persistent publisher and writer of my story. He told me that this story needed to be written and he wanted to help make it happen. My appreciation Dustin, thank you for your persistence & talent.

My executive assistant is the most talented taskmaster I have ever met. Thank you Dawnielle for keeping me on track and using your talented mastery of the printed word to help keep my voice.

I have some of the best friends in the world and I have to thank Kevin, Kendra, Danise, Teresa, my sister JoAnne and Rocco for taking their time to review and give me "the truth with love" about the book before finalizing the manuscript.

Thank you to the very talented Eric Galinger of Galinger Graphics for your tremendous vision and talent creating the dust cover design.

Most important is my husband, Tony. Yes, you are a genius and the best friend I have ever had. Our 25 year journey together did not prepare either of us for this adventure! Thank you for your constant encouragement and honest feedback always, especially during the process of writing this book.

There are many more people that have helped "write" my story through the experiences we have shared over the years. My parents, Dick and Alice Kunkel, were my first Dream Managers and I thank you and every one else for your help to make my dreams come true. My wish is that I have, or can, help you and many more see your dreams achieved.

About the Authors

MARY MILLER is the CEO of JANCOA Janitorial Services, a local certified WBE that is family owned and operated. Mary is known for her positive outlook and desire to help others realize their uniqueness and personal power. Mary has become the backbone and driving force behind the success of the company.

In addition to running a business with more than 500 full-time employees, she is an associate coach for Strategic Coach where she works with fellow entrepreneurs on concepts to focus and balance their careers with life and increase income, while working less and enjoying the process.

Mary has become a popular speaker with an international following. Mary's recent achievements include being named the 2016 Kent Clapp CEO Leadership Award winner, a 2015 Enterprising Woman of the Year and a 2013 YWCA Career Women of Achievement honoree.

Mary and her husband, Tony, have five children and nine grandchildren. When not enjoying time with family in the city, Mary and Tony enjoy the serenity of their lake home.

DUSTIN SCOTT KLEIN is an award-winning business journalist, best-selling author and the publisher and COO of *Smart Business*. Over the past 25 years Dustin has interviewed thousands of business and civic leaders, and helped nearly 30 CEOs and entrepreneurs transform their ideas into books. Six of his books were Amazon best-sellers, two of which achieved No. 1 best-seller status. Dustin lives in Shaker Heights, Ohio, with his wife, Laura, and children, Sam, Cole, and Mollie.